Breaking Through

Implementing Customer Focus in Enterprises

Sandra Vandermerwe

First published 2004 by
PALGRAVE MACMILLAN
Houndmills, Basingstoke, Hampshire RG21 6XS and
175 Fifth Avenue, New York, N.Y. 10010
Companies and representatives throughout the world

PALGRAVE MACMILLAN is the global academic imprint of the Palgrave Macmillan division of St. Martin's Press, LLC and of Palgrave Macmillan Ltd. Macmillan® is a registered trademark in the United States, United Kingdom and other countries. Palgrave is a registered trademark in the European Union and other countries.

ISBN 1–4039–3503–3

This book is printed on paper suitable for recycling and made from fully managed and sustained forest sources.

A catalogue record for this book is available from the British Library.

A catalog record for this book is available from the Library of Congress.

10 9 8 7 6 5 4 3 2 1
13 12 11 10 09 08 07 06 05 04

Printed and bound in Great Britain by
Creative Print & Design (Wales), Ebbw Vale

CONTENTS

Figures

TABLES

BOXES

We're looking outside the box, because the box we've been looking into is empty.[1]
Banking Executive, United States

Customer focus is undeniably critical in helping enterprises to grow now and into the future. Research figures prove it; corporate experience demonstrates it; and managerial insight corroborates it. In today's competitive environment, products and services – no matter how good or innovative they may be – can only produce short-lived rewards: they diminish in value over time, unlike customers who, with time, *increase* in value.[2]

There is only one way to gain lasting success: enterprises must fundamentally transform themselves so that customer focus becomes entrenched throughout the organization, shaping attitudes, priorities, and behaviour.

So it is ironic that while the importance of the customer-focused approach is irrefutable, actually making it happen remains a conundrum for most executives.

The spate of readily available, off-the-shelf customer relationship management (CRM) and loyalty packages – which executives believed in sincerely and paid for dearly – have come nowhere near to bringing the promised returns, because they don't make the fundamental changes necessary if an organization is to reap the deep and long-lasting rewards of customer focus. In the end, customers only continue to do with the enterprise what they have always done in the past. And with new products, however radical, being copied so fast they hardly have time to make their impact felt in the marketplace or on the bottom line, executives find themselves even more perplexed by the urgent challenges of understanding exactly *what* customer focus really means, and *how* to go about achieving it in order to keep their organizations prosperous and ahead of the competition.

Becoming Indispensable to Customers

The cornerstone of customer focus lies in the ability to create a different – better, quicker, easier – way of doing things for customers. It's not that products and services are unimportant, it's simply that they are no more than a means to an end. Once the end has been decided, then (and only then) can the enterprise begin to reconstruct itself so that it can become indispensable to customers in attaining this end or outcome. This is something firms have never before had to be concerned about, or learn to do, in order to enjoy success and an illustrious future.

The reason becoming indispensable to attaining an outcome is so important is that once an enterprise achieves this, customers will 'lock on' to it and come back again and again, spending more with that enterprise and costing it less. This is what leads to the opportunities for profitable, even exponential, growth. Equally important, it is the only real barrier to competitive entry: having more products (or services) or more sites, or more stores, or more factories, or more companies can never achieve this.

Nevertheless, most enterprises still try to grow by putting more or better products and services into the pipeline,[3] equating this with innovation, or they try to grow by external means such as acquisitions and mergers, most of which fail miserably, with shareholders often losing more than they gain.[4]

Why is this, when instead they could be growing through internal renewal, aimed at cementing and leveraging from relationships with customers, old and new? This is the only way enterprises will be able to sustainably outpace others: both newcomers who appear out of nowhere to make the groundbreaking changes, take the limelight, the customer base and the new wealth, and the traditional players, leaving them to deal with the whims of disenchanted customers and the ups and downs of business cycles and share prices, like any other commodity provider, branded or not.

Brains, Brawn and Balance

Many executives have intuitively grasped this concept, as well as the fact that, like most purposeful innovation, real customer focus requires fundamental change and commitment. What has held them back from putting it into practice has been the lack of a systematic process that gets the organization to make the leap, pull people out of their old set thinking and then take them along the journey to a true and enduring customer culture.

Such a process has to do two things simultaneously. It needs to spark the creativity and imagination necessary to see and chart these new ways of doing things without the comfort of hard facts, as unnerving as that may be – 'You can't research your way into the future.' You need to rely on intuition and foresight, imagination and discovery, persistence and the courage of only a few select people's conviction at the beginning. Not everyone will see or feel the opportunity or want to move into uncharted territory, dealing in futures that have not yet happened and for which neither data nor proof yet exists.

At the same time, the process should provide the structure and discipline necessary to counterweight this creativity and intuition. Achieving the right balance is fundamental to getting the resulting customer-focused ideas and insights widely understood and intrinsically accepted, making sure that people don't fall back into their old product moulds. It also ensures that sufficient momentum is gathered to put and keep the enterprise in front, outpacing competitors and able to continue exploiting a future it itself may have to create.

Fusing Strategy and Implementation

However, before this process can even start, executives must first be willing to abandon a longstanding corporate orthodoxy: the mistaken yet firmly held belief that strategy and implementation are two distinct activities, with implementation beginning only once the strategy has been formalized and finalized. This tenet inevitably leads to a disconnect, since those charged with implementing the strategy will lack the deep, rational understanding, as well as the emotional commitment, to actually drive the energy that spurs people on further. This lack is lethal for any kind of strategic initiative, but especially when trying to embed the customer approach into an organization, which ultimately requires everyone's wholehearted involvement.

In reality, the articulation of a strategy and its implementation are part of one interconnected and reiterative process, with each element reinforcing and nurturing the other. The moment people see the need for a different direction, have been tempted out to play, start to build the strategy, and make the vital moves – implementation has begun.

And once the new approach begins to take root in the market, more people in the enterprise become more confident, start looking for more opportunities, building more expertise, achieving more victories, so drawing others in, propelling the implementation further forward at an ever faster pace, as the necessary breakthroughs from one phase to the next are made.

Energizing Through Positivity

This raises another orthodoxy that needs to be conquered: executives count on resistance happening, and not without good reason. There will always be resistance to a new order – it's part of human nature. A change to customer focus in particular can raise all sorts of questions and fears, because people identify with product categories, are structured into product silos and are often rewarded accordingly, even at the very highest level in organizations.

Besides, in general, enterprises have more faith in product than customer longevity; another irony, given how slim the time advantage of products and services, even the most radical, can be today.

When too much energy, resources and focus go into dealing with the resistors and what they are resisting – instead of moving the enterprise ahead, gripped by positive energy that builds the tempo and pace that make customer focus viable, especially at the outset, when the enterprise may be precariously poised in its approach to the new beginning – a stubbornly negative pattern sets in, with forces so strong they can stall and even compromise the entire endeavour. No matter how well articulated, how finely formulated, or how critical to the enterprise's future it is, customer focus under such conditions will be slow to take off, if it leaves the ground at all.

Working with positive energy or 'points of light' has the reverse effect: people feel excited and enthused and so actively seek out opportunities instead of merely making episodic changes when it's obvious they are in trouble. 'Points of light' are individuals who not only conceptualize a new market configuration and 'get it' quickly, but want to be the ones to 'make it happen'. The energy of their actions and the strength of their convictions and strong intrinsic belief in customer focus as the route to lucrative and long-lasting growth inspire others, 360 degrees up, down and sideways in the organization.

Their positive energy is also self-reinforcing: more and more people are enticed in as the implementation progresses, bringing in its wake ever more new opportunities as confidence is gained and as successes are demonstrated and declared, giving impetus to the customer approach and motivating the implementation still further.

The Customer Focus Process

The process of achieving customer focus can be mapped into five overlapping phases. Each has its own time frame, marked by a pair of critical breakthroughs (see Exhibit 1). The ten step-by-step breakthroughs punctuating these phases are remarkably consistent across enterprises and industries. They help energize people along the way until sufficient momentum has been reached to reap and sustain the rewards.

This book will guide readers through the customer focus process, which usually takes anywhere from 18 months to 3 years, sometimes even stretching to 5 depending on the circumstances and starting point. The impetus for some could be a dire crisis; for others changing environments and pressure from deteriorating financials; some will proactively see, sense and seek growth opportunities they can't resist, while

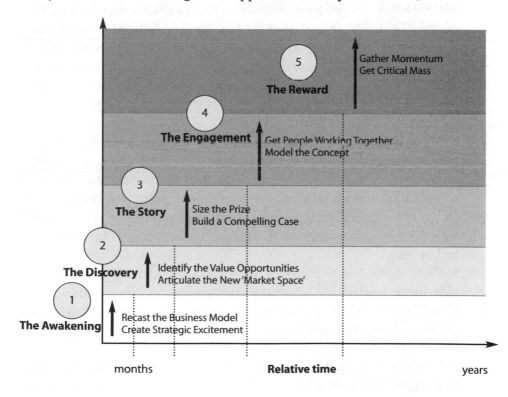

Exhibit 1 Phases and breakthroughs

others will be starting from scratch, taking advantage of the lacklustre approach to customers in heritage industries.

The book is organized into each of the five phases with emphasis on the critical success factors that create the ten breakthroughs or milestones that finally lead the enterprise to full and lasting implementation. It is from this kind of implementation that customer focus becomes imprinted into the culture of an enterprise so that it can continue to refresh and remake itself.

Background and Acknowledgements

For several decades I have watched and been part of customer-focused transformations in various capacities – as an academic researcher and consultant – in the private and public sectors.

The research began at IMD Switzerland in the mid-1980s with the development of the customer activity cycle – a tool now used in corporations worldwide – to identify gaps in the customer experience and fill these gaps to produce customer outcomes. This was followed by another research period at the Management School (now Tanaka Business School) Imperial College London from the mid-1990s to gain more insight into how corporations were transforming themselves from products to customers and using the customer activity cycle to build new offerings and the structures, technology, skills and partnering to deliver them.

More recently, it became obvious that whilst customer focus was achieving more attention by practitioners, implementation was a huge challenge. It required change management that embraced the entire organization and a transformation specifically geared to produce value from customers rather than from short-lived product or service innovation. Only then could new wealth and lasting success be created for an enterprise.

This began a new phase of the research that set out to model a systematic process for achieving customer focus. The result was the identification of the specific breakthrough actions needed to implement customer-focused transformation that forms the basis of this book.

Like most books this one draws on management literature, history and other published material. It brings together the overlapping and sometimes divergent theories of innovation, disruption theories, market orientation, strategy, change management, growth economics, services management and new accounting – all of which are relevant to reconstructing or refreshing an organization if it wants to truly become customer focused.

To those who have supported my work, inviting me into their organizations to watch and participate, to research and record, to those who listened when they weren't sure and trusted me when the stakes were high, not only for them personally but also for their enterprises, I am very grateful – for they are truly 'points of light'.

I have deliberately chosen a geographic and industry spread of examples that range from start-ups (some new, some now very well established) – all of which, with limited resources, used customer-focused principles from the outset to enter and transform staid industries – through medium-sized enterprises to large organizations in highly complex and diverse environments. For some the transformation was a total remaking of the organization because it had reached a crisis point, while others rejuvenated themselves and continue to do so through a customer-focused approach.

Irrespective of the route they took I am indebted to them, for without their collaboration this book would have been impossible and others could not have benefited from their experiences.

This work is based on applied action-based research with enterprises, and observation. In this type of research concepts and tools are developed, tested and refined to build and describe collective best practice and then articulate and make it transferable and useful to others while it is happening. I hope I have captured the key learnings – both good and bad – from this cadre of people who have and continue to influence and invent our markets and our worlds.

Other thank-yous are due to Marika Taishoff, for help with the compilation of material, referencing and editing, and to my marvellous, inspiring, ever-loving family, to whom I dedicate this work, because without them nothing would have meaning.

Finally, all quotations are genuine. Some are attributed, others remain anonymous to protect the individuals' privacy. Either way, the responsibility for interpretation is entirely mine.

The Awakening

1

The Awakening

Recast the Business Model
Create Strategic Excitement

months   **Relative time**   years

Create Strategic Excitement

Why the Mighty Fall

The most important part of the awakening to customer focus within an organization is not only that sufficient numbers of the correct people feel an urgent need for change, but, in particular, that there is an excitement about how adopting a customer approach will mean success to their enterprise now and in the long run. Without this, as many commentators and executives reiterate over and over again, there can be no real change towards sustainable growth.

Yet what's amazing is that all too often this sense of urgency and an awareness that the organization needs to be refreshed or transformed if it is to continue to flourish are starkly lacking. Not pressed to find and make opportunities to create new wealth, executives are surprised when their enterprises flounder.

We only have to look at history.

For over 100 years Marks & Spencer was almost as well known as the British Royal Family. What is more, it had spread its tentacles way beyond the British Isles to become a prominent retailer in Europe, Asia and America. Representing the world's most profitable retailer for over 50 years, the M&S brand seemed to be on its way to becoming as popular globally as it was at home, where it had supplied the UK population with a quarter of their suits, almost all their underwear and a third of their sandwiches! The centenarian institution had been voted by its peers as having the most admired management in Europe, and Harvard Business School epitomized it in a case study as one of the world's greatest companies – the only retailer in Europe to have achieved double-digit market share along with a stock price that had outperformed the market for decades.[5]

Then came the crisis...

As financials deteriorated, customers started to leave in droves. What had at one time been considered *the* brand suddenly became passé. A downward spiral followed: the more the customers left, the worse the financials became, so the more the customers left.

The same thing happened to IBM in the 1990s.

In both cases, losses were massive and swift. But more mystifying than anything else was that the trauma hit investors, the board, management and employees totally, and equally, unexpectedly.

Orthodoxies Become Heresies

How, we have to ask ourselves, can such a thing happen – to even the mightiest of players? Some argue that it's inevitable. Heritage enterprises, especially (but not exclusively) the larger ones, merely get too rigid to recreate themselves or the markets they serve. They become incapable of sensing danger or seeing opportunities that are groundbreaking because these are too far removed from their closely held notions of what constitutes success.

Worse, because they are wedded to conventional product orthodoxies, the criteria that executives use to make decisions about the future of the enterprise or to judge its performance and that of the people within it – including themselves – may actively work against customer focus and thus against realizing real growth.

In such cases, when something is actually done about customers it's more often than not at the fringes only: a new loyalty card, a customer relationship management (CRM) programme, a promotional campaign based on making and selling more of the same, just like everyone else. Wouldn't it be better to raise executives' levels of consciousness to explore new possibilities for customer potential, accept the necessary challenges associated with them, and undergo the enterprise and industry transformations fundamental to exploit these opportunities successfully?

So instead of leading markets to new places, the enterprise remains uninspired and uninspiring, staying where the markets have been. Both Marks & Spencer and IBM, from very different industries, were by their own admission totally product focused, a factor that led to their near demise. Nevertheless, both realized, just in time, that only a customer approach could work if they were to sustainably reconstruct themselves.

They and many others like them had become trapped by their success, with triumphs codified in a set of procedures that became the values by which people lived or died, the mantra, 'the way things are done around here'.

So stuck were they in the ways that had worked so wonderfully well in the past that people lived inside what executives at IBM described as a 'comfy cocoon'.[6] Whatever didn't fit inside this cocoon was either discarded, or simply didn't resonate loudly enough to be heard or to break through.

In such situations – which still abound – resources are allocated to 'what we do' as opposed to 'how we should change what we do', and to 'what we could do better inside the enterprise' rather than 'what new things we should be doing outside the enterprise for customers'.

What these and other cases remind us of is that a glorious past does not guarantee a prosperous future for an enterprise in either the private or public sector. Unless people see that doing something different – not more of the same, only better – is what will enable them to enhance their market power and give them the sensitivity and stamina to grow and keep growing, they will never make the first breakthrough needed to move forward.

Hiding Behind the Numbers

Marks & Spencer was the first retailer in the UK to make a billion pounds in profit. So no one guessed that it was in trouble and that new competitors were closing in. As one executive remarked: 'We thought profits and growth would never go away.'

The problem was that this gigantic profit wasn't coming from superior retailing for customers. In its desire to grow by getting physically bigger by doing more of the same, M&S had invested in out-of-town shopping centres instead of looking at extracting more from customers in the high streets. With itself as the magnate, it had effectively become a property owner, not a retailer, let alone a contemporary retailer.

McDonald's was no different. As the century turned, the hamburger legend had become more of a landlord than a fast-food chain, making more money from rents than from the burgers and fries that customers had long grown weary of, despite the company having one of the most gigantic promotional and advertising budgets in the world.

Part of its solution came from entrepreneur Stelios Haji-Ioannou of 'easy everything' Euro-fame, who saw things differently. In trying to resuscitate his Internet café, which was attracting 1.5 million people a month by 2003, he decided to rent unutilized space in McDonald's stores. This was part of his push to become a public utility, getting into small, stand-alone public places like airports, libraries, hotels, bus stations, restaurants and movie houses, in the process changing the reason people go to certain venues.

So no longer do customers walk into McDonald's only to buy a hamburger, they can buy time on the Web! That might have helped with McDonald's excess space, but it nevertheless exacerbated the problem that earnings were coming from rent from property, instead of spend from customers.

How Accounting Aggravates

Part of the reason that executives and others are caught unawares by problems, making the process of getting to customer focus a non-starter, is that the figures easily disguise the truth about how well an enterprise is doing. Thus the powers that be are kept in the dark, rather than being alerted to and pressed by the need for change.

In conventional terms the figures may indeed look good and make everyone feel safe, yet they may hide how far the enterprise has allowed itself to move away from its customers and from the new market trends. An outsider moving in can then be destined to change the balance of power.

Accounting and reporting conventions aggravate the situation. Instead of the figures being a window to opportunities and a warning of risks ahead, they leave the unsuspecting or uninitiated unaware and unquestioning.

As an example, let's take the lumping together of companies into sectors to compare performance ratings. This makes little sense when the real competitive threat is likely to come from without rather than within the industry, which typically happens when the focus shifts from products to customers.

For instance, banks today are facing much fiercer competition from non-banks, ranging from supermarkets to brokerage firms, and from new, innovative players like Virgin One, than from traditional players. Oil companies find that some of the large retailers, like Tesco in the UK and Wal-Mart in the United States, are now selling as much and even more petrol and lubricants to customers than they are, to cite just two simple examples.

Or again, it's not airline caterers that other caterers have to fear. Their biggest problem is that fewer people are eating in flight or that more would happily bypass meals than eat tasteless 'plastic' food.[7] Others are increasingly bringing their own 'airline picnics' along from departing hotels or picking up fresh sandwiches from fast-food retailers en route and in the airports, or simply grabbing an apple or snack to munch on while they work on their laptops during the journey.

Lumping dot.coms into a sector is another dramatic example of flawed thinking and reporting that left executives oblivious, for instance, of amazon's ultimate impact. Categorized as an internet stock, it was rated and evaluated against other internet stocks, instead of being seen for what it really was: an aggressive customer-focused on-line book store that, once it had captured the imagination and purses of customers, became a multifaceted retailer, destined to change the power base within its various sectors.

Blinding Obsessions

All sorts of accounting conventions encourage obsessions and short-term behaviour, which block awareness and the longer-term commitments necessary to get a corporation to feel the need to move from a product to a customer approach. This is despite research consistently showing that what keeps the most admired enterprises ahead of the others is their refusal to compromise long-term goals for short-term demands.[8]

Obsession with immediacy

The obsession with immediacy, which is part of the product culture where returns are expected to happen quickly, is of course transferred into reporting. Because costs and revenues are tightly squeezed into the same short time period, what people ask is 'How much are we getting from the various products in their respective silos now?' rather than 'How much are we getting from customers and are likely to get in the long run?'

Boots disposed of its 'wellbeing' idea in 2003, keeping only the traditionally profitable product lines like optics, dental care and foot care services that had shown profits while the 'wellness' initiative had accumulated losses of £75 million. However, the number of people who had signed up for the Boots Advantage card had grown to 14 million customers, of which 8 million were buying regularly – an investment in acquisition that probably cost the company between £5 and £9 per customer. That's a small price to pay for the kind of potential that could have stretched far into the future had a unified customer approach been the intention and carried through.[9]

Amazon could have made a profit long before it did, but Jeff Bezos chose not to as he sturdily built the platform from which to capitalize later on. Some investors realized this ('to me the company's losses are a sign of health not sickness') and others didn't.[10] At the height of the controversy Bezos maintained his cool and his stand against the heavy anti-amazon contingent. Here are two of his now classic quotes, which are worth repeating:[11]

We have always taken great pains to urge investors who have a short term investment horizon not to invest in our stock.

The company is not the stock ... when the stock was booming we had 14 million customers ... in 2000 when the stock was busting we had about 20 million customers buying from us.

Obsession with market share

When the world was getting ready for the new millennium, Lego had a world market share in building construction toys of over 70 per cent, in Europe just on 90 per cent. But thanks to a combination of demographics – like low birth rates – and competitive and technological phenomena – such as ever shorter product life spans and the proliferation of computers, videos and media games – Lego had lost share of kids' playing time. This is a showcase example of how market share may look good while really saying nothing about markets, only about product categories, and still less about how well the company may fare in a future that has already begun to make its impact felt.

The real point is this: for as long as an enterprise aims at mere market share, it will simply get share of product, not share of customer.

And so while data in conventional reporting can make an organization seem to be moving forward because it meets product/market share targets, it may be standing still or even reversing because it is either getting a larger piece of a diminishing market, as was the case with Lego's share of kids' playing time, or only a small piece of a growing market, as happened to IBM in the 1990s when top management rejected every opportunity that wasn't about making and moving their 'boxes'.

Obsession with the bottom line

Managing the bottom line is fundamental to keeping any enterprise economically viable. But all too often the product culture that gives this its main attention confuses the need for operational efficiency with the need to build capabilities to excel in a new world.

The highly scrutinized product numbers tell no tale of impending trends that may ultimately make or break the business. And to get numbers up, emphasis is often given to increasing margins through cost cutting. That is problematic if these profits are achieved to the detriment of building market power and long-term customer wealth, which is what happens when cost-cutting efforts are done in isolation, without customer focus at the core. From one executive comes this remark: 'We had someone get the president's prize for reducing the supply chain costs by x per cent of sales. Meanwhile the reduction in inventory cost us much more – it destroyed our image and relationship with customers which took us years to recover.'

One of the most serious problems with bottom-line obsession is that enterprises miss out on the new wealth, either because they are not looking for it, or because they choose to ignore it, or because they believe that it takes them too far outside the core businesses they are so desperately trying to optimize.

IBM's blue, so to speak, was that it failed to see that by sticking to the 'boxes' it was losing out on the new wealth. No matter how good

---

Box 1.1 Financials to trigger an awakening

Good company earnings, without commensurate top-line growth

Good consistent profits, without aggressive investments in customer innovations

Revenues slipping though profits are up

Market shares high in product categories where the market is changing direction or slowing down

Profits good but competition coming increasingly from outside the industry

Growth from recovery, not real growth

Revenues mainly from price-driven deals and performance

Ambitious geographic expansion without a real customer edge

Mergers and acquisitions to grow market share, but unlikely to lead to a changed marketplace

---

they were, these IBM 'boxes' were trivial in the life of customers who wanted fully functioning networking capability and didn't know where to begin to make it happen. So while IBM continued to fight for 10 per cent of the spend on these, 90 per cent of the new money went to outsiders who created whole industries around helping customers make that capability happen, an opportunity IBM either didn't see or deliberately decided it didn't want to be part of.

If profits are not accompanied by increases in the top line, representing real growth (as opposed to just buying more share of an existing market), it's a clear signal that the enterprise is out of touch with the marketplace. In Box 1.1 are some of the more classic financial scenarios that are indicative of this and can be used at the awakening phase to provoke dialogue and trigger the need for a new perspective.

Raising Aspirations

Of course, not all enterprises need a crisis or a fall to leave the product mould and become customer focused. They can become aware just in time that the customer approach is more resilient for a future where pressure mounts as dramatic changes in the environment threaten to destroy not only their market power, but perhaps that of the whole industry as well.

Usually by that time the numbers or key ratios have already begun to slacken, because most executives still tend to focus on the figures before they look at the market. But that doesn't stop them taking the measures to make people aware that the business model has to be altered to focus on customers and their long-term and longer-lasting rewards, rather than on making, buying and selling products that eventually lead to diminishing returns.

This is what happened to information and news business Lexis Nexis, when customers began to shave their budgets for content publications in protest against the plethora of information being sold to them. Much of this information was freely or cheaply available over the Web in any case, so customers in both the private and public sectors began to do their own research, making traditional providers less and less relevant in their lives and professions.

Making people feel uncomfortable is easy, especially when the enterprise has reached a crisis point or the numbers have deteriorated. This helps to ignite the spark required for any serious change.

The discomfort will come from people's fear that new thinkers with younger, fresher brands will steal their customers and potentially downgrade their products and services into commodities, despite their size. The signs may already be evident in falling margins, lost deals, customer fall-off, lack of contract renewal and, most importantly, defection of customers to brands from outside the industry.

Opening Up New Horizons

What is much more difficult, yet also more rewarding, is instilling a sense of strategic excitement about the prospects for renewed growth and vitality made possible by the customer focus model showing clear intent to transform the company via a new direction so that people feel positive and inspired rather than fearful and defensive. This is the route that was taken by Bill Pardue, President of Lexis Nexis's US Corporate and Federal Market Division.

Past behaviour at Lexis Nexis would have been to look for more innovative content to publish, as well as attempting to cut costs and somehow hold on to its existing market share. Pardue instinctively knew not only that this approach would fail to secure the company's market position in the long term, but that it was also incapable of growing any new wealth. Instead, he got his senior team excited about the prospect that professionals who had to make decisions carrying a high degree of risk or reward – law enforcement officers, patent officials, litigating lawyers or in-house scientists – would be prepared to pay for information, as long as this information helped them make better, quicker decisions: to track down a criminal, assess a patent application, win a case or develop a breakthrough product. And Pardue's intuition was right: within three years his division had outpaced competitors, boosted customer spend and achieved surging profits.

Still others create their environment while their organizations are growing. Per Bay Jorgensen, CEO of Denmark's International Health Insurance (IHI), 'saw' in the 1970s that there was an opportunity to offer health insurance to expatriates living or retiring in countries where these services were poor. Because this didn't fit in with his predecessor's view of the brave new world, he formed a new company that has now grown to have policyholders in over 150 countries.

Later, sensing that the growth and wealth would be with 'unpatients' – people who were well and would be prepared to pay to stay that way – early in 2000 Jorgensen began to revitalize his company around the concept of helping customers – mostly high end, high value – be well, rather than merely selling them or their employees health policies. He redefined the notion of being well to include health as well as being and feeling safe while travelling and living abroad – an approach that has kept the company growing, even as others in the industry fell on hard times after the millennium.

Beyond Core Products to Core Purpose

Creating strategic excitement, rather than only discomfort and fear, means raising levels of consciousness about what is possible with a new perspective around innovating to build a new core purpose for the enterprise.

This can be pretty tough for an enterprise whose capabilities have revolved around making, buying and selling products such as published content, health insurance policies, or Lego's construction bricks – named 'Toy of the Century' by *Fortune* magazine in 1999 – which had been their building blocks to success for decades.

That is why *people's* aspirations, not merely those of the enterprise, have to be changed. At Lego for instance, where the biggest problem in the 1980s was managing demand for its bricks and controlling growth, the most daunting challenge was to get the people in the enterprise to see that while the growth potential for their bricks was limited, the opportunities to enhance the quality of customers' play experiences were limitless. So rather than simply continuing to perfect its physical bricks as in the past, Lego's transformation was built around merging the physical and virtual worlds to enable kids to foster their creativity, conceptual thinking, interactive learning and sense of fun while at play (the Danish words 'leg godt', after which the company was named, mean play well).

Going Against Customer Orthodoxies

Customer aspirations may also have to be changed. One of the great marketing fallacies holding back true customer focus is the belief that customers know what they want and can (and would) articulate it, if only they were asked, using traditional research methods. This isn't so (let's never forget that a reputable research company told IBM that there would be no demand for mini-computers!). Were it so, customers, not enterprises, would be creating the future and executives would be reacting to requests rather than inventing markets, inching forward instead of making the groundbreaking changes that positively transform the lives of customers and themselves.

In fact, many of the great transformations require enterprises to go against customer orthodoxies. Baxter Healthcare Germany made such a leap when it moved from selling post-operative prod-ucts to hospitals to creating a way for patients who had had life-threatening diseases to rehabilitate at home. The country manager had argued that patients would be better off with post-operative care at home rather than in hospital. Until then, doctors kept patients in hospital as long as possible and, once back home, patients were only provided with the basics like nursing and wheel-chairs, from a variety of providers. The real breakthrough came when Baxter executives began to see that this new approach to rehabilitation made sense and they wanted to be the ones to make it a reality.

People who awaken organizations and then take them along a systematic process to become customer focused typically trust their intuition about markets and where they are going, or could go. 'Though on paper things may not be perfect or 100 per cent clear or obvious, they feel right' is how they describe this.

They don't spend fortunes on analysing transactional data in the hope that that will reveal the big new idea, or on crunching the numbers to find the proof that the market indisputably exists. These executives acknowledge that what they are looking for isn't in the figures, and the uncharted territories they are about to create don't yet exist.

Instead, they work with 'educated intuition' to formulate a new direction for the enterprise. They form a hypothesis or proposition about how the world could look were they to take this new direction, which they may see and others may not. They explore it, examine it, and let it evolve into something meaningful with those whose support they are trying to win at the outset.

That's not to say that they don't do any research at all. However, the research is to help awaken the organization by giving credence to the hypothesis, and add substance and legs to speed the process along, rather than expecting customers to tell them what to do.

Finding 'Points of Light'

When the strategic excitement comes from the top of an organization, so much the better. In fact, most people who have been through a customer focus process – or failed to get one off the ground – say that unless the chief executive officer (CEO) drives it, the change from product to customer will simply never materialize.

In practical terms, this is probably true when an enterprise is in crisis or forced to adapt to some serious environmental or technological disruption. Here, executives say, the CEO must be visibly seen out front, pushing the endeavour and claiming responsibility for doing whatever they say is urgently needed for the organization to change.

If the transformation is not fraught with this kind of trauma, however, the force for change can come from people other than the CEO, provided they are senior enough and have credibility. 'Just five years ago,' remarked one executive, 'it would have *had* to be the CEO leading the customer focus for anyone to listen – but not today: so long as someone with influence and able to enthuse people is making the case, it can work.'

Luckily these individuals are now more tolerated, even appreciated. Top management are willing to allow people with insight and hunger to get on with things, and their fresh, unorthodox views of where the enterprise should be going and what it should be doing to get there are encouraged and admired rather than ignored or punished as in the old days.

The Consensus Myth

This is a significant shift from the past, when change had to be cascaded downwards in an organization.

Nevertheless, one of the important questions that people at the forefront of making new things happen have to ask is: how many people should we involve, and who? This has to be resolved early on if leaders are going to be able to move the process forward with gusto and tempo, and to do so in a positive way, enlightening rather than frightening, inspiring rather than ordering.

The temptation has always been to have as large a group as possible. But executives have learned the hard way that including too many of the wrong people invariably means having to waste time and effort on those who obstinately resist anything new until they see it concretely demonstrated.

So executives should actively look for and work with 'points of light' – when they do, they will achieve the breakthroughs. Not only does not having to continually encounter and counter points of resistance conserve time and effort, but it speeds up the process and ensures that the energy level remains high enough to carry it forward, especially at this crucial point.

The alternative, which is involving too many people or the wrong people at the outset when the new direction is still fresh and being formulated, can be a hindrance and even a hold-up, setting a negative pattern of having to continuously break down resistance instead of building up enthusiasm and pace.

Executives still have to deal with resistance – it's a normal part of any change process. But when all of the time and energy goes into this resistance it can damage, delay or permanently derail the customer focus process, particularly at this early phase.

Part of the reason this has happened in the past is that cascading down meant it was necessary to achieve consensus, especially from the senior ranks. However, what history has taught us is that seniority guarantees neither sensitivity to markets nor a willingness to change. In trying to get this consensus, executives have had to use a disproportionate amount of effort battling with objectors and objections instead of working with positive forces that propel a customer focus journey forwards.

So increasingly enterprises are learning that to move the process along successfully, they need to avoid what Rosabeth Moss Kanter calls the inevitable 'knee-jerk no's',[12] a particularly prevalent reaction with customer-focused transformation because concepts cannot be well articulated until they have been more clearly defined and seen in action.

In addition, they have had to learn to distinguish between those people and perspectives that are relevant, and those that are not. The following remarks come from people who have been through it:

There are some people you take with you and others you just can't touch ...

It could have been quicker if we hadn't spent so much time trying to convince people who were inconvincible, and just got on with it.

Typical refrains from the resistors include:

Tell me who has done this before in our industry.

We have done this before and failed miserably.

We don't have the capabilities.

The timing is all wrong.

Our business is different.

We barely have enough resources to cope with day-to-day problems.

How does this fit in with our existing strategic plans?

Moving Ahead with Positive Energy

Rather than spending precious resources on breaking down the 'points of resistance', leaders actively look for 'points of light'. These people are more than just innovators who take on new ideas first. They become the fulcrum for drawing others into the process and managing the projects that take it and them forward and through to fruition.

While resistors want to hang onto the past, 'points of light' see the opportunities and recognize that to make an impact, they have to make a difference to customers' lives. While resistors tend to be negative and put emphasis on the problems, 'points of light' are positive, find a way around problems and want to be part of making changes happen.

'Points of light' are energizers who are able to inspire others, unlike resistors who drain energy and conspire with others to block change – either consciously or unconsciously.[13] Able to use their personal and political capital to influence others, 'points of light' expand and spread this energy through 360 degrees in the organization, so propelling the implementation on.

Whereas resistors are usually stuck in silos, continually concerned about their own turf and the ramifications of change on it and their stature and personal range of influence, 'points of light' see how people fit into the bigger picture and constructively work to make sure that everyone gains. That is why they are beacons, and others gravitate into their orbit and to their ideas.

Most important, 'points of light' are equally comfortable with what can be a paradox: using creativity and imagination to find the future, while having the structure and discipline to get there, which is critical to making the process of customer focus work.

Recast the Business Model

Grounding Theory into Practice

Without a deep grounding in why customer focus is the business model to follow and what it means, there won't be the emotional or cognitive understanding that is needed to take the process the next step. As practitioners and the literature have recently emphasized, both these components are important if any meaningful change is to occur. People have to feel the need to do things differently and be exposed to problems at first hand rather than merely be told or persuaded on a purely rational basis. The latter was the case only a decade ago when change initiatives were regimented and people obeyed as they responded to, rather than invented, the environment.

An induction period of a few days, weeks or months, depending on the number of people and geographies involved, is therefore an essential ingredient of moving customer focus forward. When the new approach appeals to them both emotionally and rationally, people are prepared to break with the past, even excited about it. To work effectively on both the emotional and rational levels nevertheless requires a new perspective and view to be presented so that individuals feel they can enter the future with enthusiasm.

Also needed is a deep understanding of why people have to deal differently with customers, what they have to do, and the rewards this will bring. It is only then that they really begin to feel ready to proceed comfortably and confidently.

This is where the theory fits in. The word theory is enough to make most executives shudder, wary that it may never work in real life. Yet most management actions are based on theory: assumptions made about cause and effect, or connections that get enterprises and the people within them to a desired place and result if they behave in a particular way.

The theory underlying customer focus puts the customer approach into perspective. And distinguishes it from the product approach which most enterprises practice though they may not think they do.

Not only do the high-level principles and concepts act as stimulants because they show how the new way is more advantageous than the old, but they become the guiding forces for the decisions people have to make as they move along the process.

The 'Whys' Behind the 'Whats'

So, how the past is different from the future, old notions that should be replaced by fresh contemporary ideas, and how the locus and focus of value must change are all part of the agenda that enables the business model to be recast from products to customers at this awakening phase. Without some time devoted to this, the process will lack the necessary grounding to evolve further: people will end up struggling more than is necessary, it will take more time, and the initial excitement generated will in all likelihood wither away.

More distressing is that without this breakthrough – namely when people not only understand why they have to discard their old assumptions but also feel enthusiastic about adopting something fresh and more relevant to a customer approach, even though still untried – they will revert to old thinking and behaviour patterns and it will be difficult, if it is even possible, to recreate the initial bursts of enthusiasm and energy.

New high-level principles and concepts also need to be shared so that people from different parts of the organization can go through the various phases of customer focus together. Interventions provide a forum for building a common view and language that align people to customers and to each other, as well as allowing a collective spirit to emerge.

Most importantly, these new precepts and concepts help people to formulate the customer concept and communicate it to others. They may be positive and motivated, but they may never before have had to confront the challenges that lie ahead, or express in any formal way what they intuitively feel. They also need help to work with quite a different set of people and make this journey together. 'Only when we spent time doing this kind of stuff could we then discuss unfamiliar territory in a familiar way.'

Turning the Product Corner

An essential part of the awakening is getting people to see that future wealth for the enterprise must come from extracting value from customers rather than from products. In addition, they need to realize that the product model is limited because its advantages are short lived. More and better products (or services, for that matter) – however good or innovative – cannot in and of themselves give an enterprise a competitive edge, because someone will always copy them and have better/cheaper ones to sell.

PRINCIPLE 1: THE VALUE OF CUSTOMERS INCREASES WITH TIME

The first high-level principle is a simple one: over time the value that products bring to an enterprise diminishes, whereas the more customer longevity the enterprise captures, the more it gains.

So the first customer focus principle can be summarized like this:

> *The value of products or services diminishes with time*
> **whereas**
> *the value of customers increases over time*

The mobile phone industry typifies this concept. Nokia, a small and insignificant Finnish pulp and paper mill, emerged out of nowhere in the late 1980s to take the centre spot in handset mobile phones and then, in the 1990s, in internet mobility. By being first, it gained the initial benefits and took the lion's share. Subsequently sales have gone up and down depending on market conditions and business cycles and competitive bombardment from traditional rivals, who unveil new handsets as quickly as Nokia does. Then came the low-cost players, who quickly incorporated new technologies into their goods and, finally, the newcomers, who arrived with yet more technological prowess in placing the internet into the palm of customers' hands.

With sophisticated marketing techniques, all of these companies parade their differences in various ways to obtain global market share. They use websites, loyalty clubs and co-branding agreements, offering teenagers special features like music on-line, games and movie images, and business customers instant retrieval of data, multimedia messages, digital pens and handwritten text messages. The assumption is that if you get in first you can ride the advantage and growth will come from replacement or new products and services, or different products for different markets that will rev up sales. If you give customers models with new or more features – like colour, design, being compact and lightweight, or flashiness pure and simple – or you move from voice to data, or from function to fun to fashion to more function to more fun to more fashion, they will buy from you; which of course they may.

Products are (Only) a Means, not an End

But is this kind of growth real and sustainable or merely winning market share one day only to lose it the next? Will customers continue to buy from enterprises and rely increasingly on them when their business model and way of doing things is product-based – easy for others to copy and even supersede? It's no surprise that the answer to this question is 'no', as the mobile phone industry and others keep reminding us.

Innovation, for these and other product-focused players, is regarded as either an incremental change to existing products or as a technological disruption, creating revolutionary new products. Instead of which innovation should really be about forging a customer approach so as to have true and long-lasting hold.

Here products and services are but a means to an end – ultimately it's this end that customers want and the enterprise has to deliver.

Most mobile phone manufacturers and operators neither know nor, it seems, particularly care, who buys their products or services. When an existing or new player finally does become the customer's mobile concierge, indispensable to individuals on the move, whether for fun, function or fashion, it will leave the others by the wayside, relegated to simply making the handsets or providing the services – and suffering the inevitable consequences. This is the fate that awaits not only the mobile phone manufacturers, but all other enterprises who continue to perpetuate the product-based business model.

With product focus, investments are made in products so the idea is to hold onto them for as long as possible, perfect them, update them, and extract as much value from them early on before the competitive onslaught hits, eroding margins and forcing investments

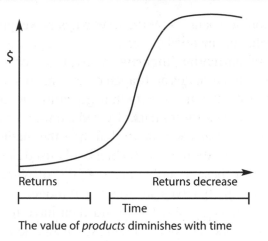

The value of *products* diminishes with time

Exhibit 2 Conceptual product curve and returns over time

to be remade, so perpetuating the classic product lifecycle treadmill (see Exhibit 2).

Even in very sophisticated markets, such as healthcare where science advances daily, no product, technology, patent or scientific merit can keep a company ahead, simply because the early advantage gained is too easy to emulate and undo.

The point to be made is this: more/better/quicker/cheaper/fancier products, or disruptive technologies, can only go so far to put an enterprise sustainably outfront. It's time for an alternative model, one based squarely on customers.

Pushing the Curve Onward and Upward

Pharmaceutical companies provide yet another example of the diminishing returns that stem from the product approach, as margins deteriorate at an ever-increasing rate. Typical priorities for such firms include the next technological breakthrough and generation of the product; the R&D investment; the speed at which it can be patented; and the rate and amount at which it must be sold to recoup development costs and satisfy return on investment (ROI) requirements.

The alternative would be to get involved in the derived needs stemming from customers: helping the healthcare fraternity achieve patient outcomes in disease areas, or even, going a step further, looking at healthy populations and seeking new ways of keeping them well and at peak performance levels.

This is of particular importance given government concerns in Europe, the United States and Japan over unnecessary hospital administration and replacement costs that governments are determined to cut, which would also dramatically reduce the number of medicines being taken. In some cases more than half the medicine prescribed is being wasted because it is unsuitable, badly used or over-prescribed.[14]

Priorities for these manufacturers – most of whom, with a product approach, see themselves as too far removed from end users to become genuinely involved – would then have to include interventions with doctors and their patients to ensure active involvement in getting good outcomes. At the top of the agenda would be consideration of the kinds of investments needed for this, and how best to exploit the new opportunity.

Irrespective of industry, when investments are made in customer outcomes – rather than in product/service innovations, which only lead to a series of transactions that soon run their course – the enterprise concentrates on how to produce and deliver real customer value, ongoing and long term. It is by doing this that the organization is able to hold onto customers, rather than products, for as long as possible. And,

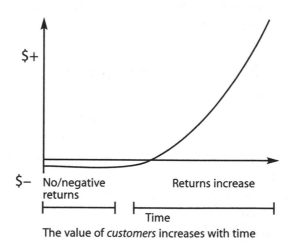

The value of *customers* increases with time

Exhibit 3 Conceptual customer curve and returns over time

in stark contrast to products, it sees how the value of these customers increases, even exponentially (see Exhibit 3).

The key to new wealth and growth today must come from extracting customer value over time, not from product transactions at a moment in time. Once an enterprise truly understands and embraces this, it will have made an important breakthrough towards becoming customer focused.

Why Customer 'Lock-On'?

Customers who 'lock on' want the enterprise as their sole or first choice over time, even over a lifetime. This is because that organization is in a better position than any other to provide the unified value that leads to an outcome for them. A powerful wake-up call comes when executives realize that, though they may have hoped differently, they don't have customer 'lock-on' because, no matter how good they are at making, buying and selling products, these come nowhere close to enabling them to achieve a desired customer outcome and thereby to be indispensable to these customers.

The Self-Reinforcing Customer 'Lock-On' Loop

When customers lock on, a self-reinforcing loop (see Exhibit 4) is set up, whereby the more the relationship grows and the more information and know-how are shared, the better the enterprise can be at understanding the needs and behaviour of individuals. As this happens the enterprise can give more value to that individual person or institution, and increase customer lock-on. This results in greater sharing of information and knowledge and in-depth profiling, which the enterprise turns to even more value, and so forth …

This is how the enterprise is able to maximize the lifetime value of individual customers, as well as attain 'contracts that continue in perpetuity' from corporate clients. Customers then become both the barrier to competitive entry and the vehicle for growth as the potential for getting longer, deeper, stronger and more diverse revenues increases.

Exhibit 4 Customer 'lock-on' loop

PRINCIPLE 2: INCREASED VALUE COMES FROM CUSTOMER 'LOCK-ON'

And so to the next principle:

> **Through customer 'lock-on'**
> *the enterprise is giving value over time*
> *and, in return,*
> *getting value over time*

Customer Lock-On is not Customer Lock-In ...

Another awakener is the realization that customer lock-on is not customer lock-in. When customers are locked in – a situation still advocated by some – they are effectively imprisoned. They either can't get out because the enterprise has a monopoly, or can't break free from some artificial legal/political/technological constraint.

This may be a very complex entanglement or very subtle. Take the Nokia mobile phone's keyboard: always the same from one Nokia model to the next, it is different enough from competitors' models to supposedly make Nokia buyers wary of having to buy another brand.

More interesting is when customers stay with the enterprise because they have no choice: the entire industry behaves in the same way, locking severely disenchanted customers in until disruptors enter, as they inevitably do, with a new way of doing things and quickly entice the customer base away, finding them only too eager.

... Nor is it Customer Loyalty

What quickly puts true customer focus in a new light is demonstrating how different it is from the customer loyalty programmes so popular with enterprises that are product driven. Organizations sometimes mistake these off-the-shelf packages, which could have paved the way for thinking more about customers, for a genuine attempt to embrace the customer approach.

Customer loyalty is primarily a product concept (see Table 2.1) aimed at achieving repeat purchasing at lower transactional costs. Even the usefulness of retention as an indicator is being re-evaluated, given that it doesn't properly distinguish between customers who bring in value and those who do not. In addition, in Frederick Reichheld's

Table 2.1 Customer loyalty versus customer 'lock-on'

	Customer loyalty	Customer lock-on
Enterprise objective	Get repeat purchases of 'stuff' to meet sales quotas	Get deeper, wider, and more diverse share of spend over longer times, even lifetimes
Method	Transactions	Interactions
Relationship	Short-term, self-involved	Long-term, reciprocal
Customer motive	Collect points, rewards	Get value
Economics	Cost of transaction goes down (old customers cost less than new)	Costs of ingredients that comprise value go down (the stronger the connection with the customer, the more the potential to reduce costs)
Requires	New systems, software and promotion	Fundamental change

words, retention 'measures the degree to which the bucket is empty-ing rather than filling up'[15] or growing.

On the other hand, customer lock-on seeks more interaction with individual customers in order to build up the information and know-how, connections and close contact that make these corporations, insti-tutions or individuals lifelong propositions. This is what gets value from an enterprise, and gives it back in return.

Research in the United States, corroborated by that done in the UK, shows that loyalty programmes rewarding customers for buying more 'stuff' have not produced the kind of results to which true customer focus aspires.[16] In fact, they don't even improve loyalty or increase average spending. (Why should they? Customers are only buying what they buy anyway, except now they're using points instead of cash!)

Customers may get a better deal, earning points or getting discounts, and so might return to that brand or store or airline for as long as the deal seems better than competitors'. However, they may not be getting the superior value or outcome that would make them true lifetime prospects, and make the enterprise impermeable to competitors.

Neither do loyalty programmes, in contrast to common belief, neces-sarily increase profitability.[17] Mistakes are difficult, and thus expen-sive, to rectify, especially when customers are already resentful because they feel they cannot easily spend their points or that promised benefits are being taken away from them.

Learning more about customers by getting sophisticated data on customer transactions and demographics, 'stalking, not wooing customers',[18] has also not produced the loyalty expected, let alone customer lock-on. In 2003, $50 billion was spent on CRM,[19] basically to improve loyalty. Unbelievably, however, 55 per cent of CRM projects drove customers away and actually diluted earnings!

No amount of money spent on loyalty programmes, CRM, or any of the other short-term traditional marketing tactics will help the corporation hold on to customers, grow their value and compete sustainably. This can only be achieved by getting customer lock-on – and that can only be accomplished by fundamentally altering the way an enterprise does business with its customers.

Research by McKinsey in the United States shows that 80 per cent of customers buying apparel, and 70 per cent of those purchasing groceries, are constantly seeking an alternative place to shop while at their chosen retailers.[20]

During the first four years of the new millennium, banks and financial institutions, who spent fortunes on CRM, failed to achieve even a single loyal customer group; in fact, overall satisfaction rates dropped. This is in startling contrast to the old days, when banking was a lock-in industry without any real outside competition. Then only 2 per cent of people were likely to switch – now two-thirds of customers say they have no loyalty to their banks and so will switch whenever it suits them.[21]

It's not difficult to see why. Had banks been prepared to back start-up companies, for instance, instead of demanding collateral when these firms were least likely to have it, venture capitalists might never have made the dent they did in the banks' markets. Ironically, eager to lend to blue-chip and larger companies at preferential rates of interest, banks soon found, sometimes too late, that these turned out to be the most risky.

Or what more potent example than the harm done to the confidence of investors –who helplessly watched the value of their portfolios deteriorate in the past five years – especially baby boomers getting ready to retire, who suddenly find themselves in the happy situation that they have the potential to live longer, but may not have the financial status to see themselves through the extra years in the financial manner to which they have been accustomed.

Individuals Lock On, Not Markets

To return to Marks & Spencer, increasingly its future is about customer lifestyle events rather than involving a series of discrete, unrelated products and services. 'It's the difference between selling the perfect Christmas pudding and getting to the customer everything that family wants to have a perfect Christmas.'

If M&S were still selling only the perfect Christmas turkey or pudding, it would use traditional marketing tools to broadcast how good the turkey or pudding is. With customer lock-on as the goal, offering the perfect Christmas to the family requires:

- trusted conversation so that customers share what they know and want
- a customer memory bank to incorporate what is already known about them
- a tight relationship so that information is shared back and forth and the customer involves the enterprise early on in the decision-making process
- interactions and discussions on options
- reactions on results to feed back into the system
- updating and constant innovation.

This gets us to another principle:

PRINCIPLE 3: CUSTOMERS ARE INDIVIDUALS WITH UNIQUE NEEDS

Products and services are aimed at average customers in a particular segment.
Outcomes are personalized for specific individuals.

There are two rules for becoming personalized. The first is to forget about an average customer, because there is no such thing – customers are diverse, even unique, and need to be treated as such.

Greek physician Hippocrates once said: 'It's more important to know what kind of person has the disease than to know what kind of disease the person has.' Evidence-based medicine may provide data about the mythical average customers and drugs, but it doesn't address the challenge that Hippocrates presented: how to minimize a specific person's risk of getting a disease, spot it early, manage it, get rid of it and minimize the chances of re-occurrence.

That is why Primary Care Trusts (PCTs) in the UK are localizing their efforts. Just a couple of years ago budgets were allocated on a national basis. Now (increasingly with the help of pharmacists) the PCTs identify most likely population problems and people per local area, and supply and manage medicines accordingly through pharmacies in that area.

Personalization is what gets customer lock-on.

Jeff Bezos had a favourite line when he (and Amazon) were still question marks in 1998: 'We know 2 per cent today of what we will know 10 years from now and most of that learning is going to revolve around personalization – the notion of making a cyber store ideal for a particular customer. If we have 4.5 million customers, we should have 4.5 million stores.'[22]

Little did his critics know that the 4.5 million customer target would only five years later become 35 million active customers who were happily – their satisfaction scores in 2003 were reportedly the highest ever, not just on-line or in retailing but in any service industry[23] – supporting the Amazon brand. They also spent 10 per cent more than did the average of all online shoppers.[24]

Nor did they know how important that remark and the behaviour it sparked would be in providing the customer lock-on that would make Amazon such a formidable player and indeed role model.

The second rule for becoming personalized is to get beyond simplistic segmentation. More and more specialized knowledge of different markets or industries is a prerequisite for gaining entry to customers and engaging them. But within these segments, specific customer types across industries may have more in common than people within industries.

It was a breakthrough for Bill Pardue's team when they realized that what a corporate lawyer does in a pharmaceutical company is more akin to what a corporate lawyer does in a consumer electronics firm than to what a researcher does in a pharmaceutical company. It was this realization that allowed the team to fathom the kinds of decisions these people had to take on a day-to-day basis, and thus the kind of information Lexis Nexis needed to provide them with.

Segmentation has traditionally relied on surveys and mass observation made at a point in time and aimed at clustering groups with similar characteristics or needs, and then tailoring offerings according to these groups. In contrast, personalization profiles the behaviour and *changing* needs of individuals, households or enterprises *over a period of time* on the basis of ongoing face-to-face or electronic interaction with them. The constant updating of databases through ever-stronger relationships and contact with customers enables these enterprises to get deeper information about them and so further intensify the connection and potential for giving and getting value.

Unifying the Customer Concept

Power lies in a unified customer concept. A unified view of the customer requires bringing together all of the bits, rather than products and services, departments, companies or even industries being seen as discrete and kept separate and separated.

This is because from the customer's point of view, they aren't separate.

Let's take banking as an example. Traditional financial enterprises and the people within them see themselves in a particular department or industry selling particular products or services. Customers have a different view of themselves: moving through the different phases of their lives, they have different liquidity needs that change and evolve.

They start (see Exhibit 5) as borrowers, perhaps students, who aspire to wealth. They then move on to find a job, start their own business, and begin to build and create wealth through savings and investment. This continues until finally they start to protect and use the wealth and then dis-save: they spend what they have, retire, and enter the final period of their lives, perhaps leaving some wealth behind to, say, children, who then become wealth inheritors.

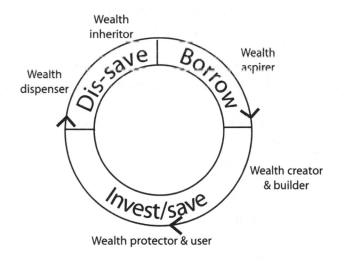

Exhibit 5 Unified customer view in life phases

In Good Times and Bad

At each of these life stages liquidity may be required for a particular reason at the very worst time: a loan for a first car when still a student; bridging finance in a small business as the economy takes a downturn; renovating a second home as the stock market turns sour.

When customers have to deal with a variety of companies and industries, each doing their own thing, it costs those customers time, effort and money. When customers are seen holistically and as lifelong prospects, the customer's position, instead of the enterprise's, can be optimized.

Some banks are beginning to underscore the importance of this unified customer view, getting rid of old rigidities. Virgin now makes efforts to help people cope with the unexpected. Customers can under-pay at certain times, break a payment schedule and pay early without penalties to suit their changing circumstances.

Other progressive financial institutions are also starting to cross over and blur traditional lines, mastering intellectually and opera-tionally this notion of a single view of the customer. Merrill Lynch, one of the leading US and international stockbrokers, decided that customers today, especially the growing numbers of baby boomers, were not only interested in the accumulation of wealth, but also in its preservation for day-to-day use, as they begin to reach the semi-retired or retired phases of their lives. As part of its total financial management plan for its customers, the stockbroker offered what it called 'Beyond Banking', which merges the artificially separated buckets of stockbroking and banking and ties them together as part of ongoing, lifetime liquidity management with a single point of customer contact.

The whole point about a unified customer concept is that the customer is better off, in good times and bad, which means that ulti-mately so is the enterprise. Virgin One consolidates loans with check-ing, savings, money market, car loan and mortgage accounts so that customers don't have to go through the costs, inconvenience and stress of having to deal with different institutions for different financial requirements. It estimates that over 25 years this saves a customer – assuming an income of £50,000 and a mortgage of £100,000 – close to £125,000.

Virgin One also pools the client's borrowings and savings in order to maximize interest on savings and minimize interest on borrowings. By bunching together into a single account all their products and customers' real balances, these virtual accounts give these customers the advantage of paying interest, or earning it, calculated on the combined accounts, when all incomings and outgoings are consolidated at the end of each business day. Consequently, large sums can be gained or saved, mortgage terms shortened and potential tax cuts on interest from savings enjoyed.

Direct Line is another outsider that entered and revolutionized the automobile insurance industry in 1985, and is now outperforming its peers, expected to soon be the largest personal lines motor insurer in the UK, repeating its success in Europe as well.

Having moved deeper into the financial services sector, it allows customers to have individual 'jam jars' corresponding to how the funds they borrow are allocated to specific goals, such as education for the kids, family vacations, home improvements and so on. However, because the amounts in all of these 'jam jars' are pooled together, customers enjoy the best overall interest rate on them. Families or friends can also put their savings into one pot and so gain from the higher rates on larger sums; up to six people can participate and still have secured private accounts.

So now we have the next customer focus principle:

PRINCIPLE 4: CUSTOMERS LOCK ON WHEN THEY GET AN OUTCOME

Products and services from enterprises, departments and industries that are separate, however good, cannot make an enterprise indispensable to customers.
Only a unified view of the customer that leads to a superior customer outcome can do this.

New Ways of Doing Things

Getting a desired outcome that spans traditional boundaries means finding ways of doing things for customers, not merely making and selling new/better/cheaper products and services. Instead, develop new ways of using information to make critical decisions; of ensuring employee wellbeing at home or on the move; of buying books; of managing energy; of managing financial liquidity.

Bezos was bound to break into the book business because book publishing, retailing and wholesaling were all industries that lacked customer focus and lustre; and customers, including Bezos, a book lover, wanted just that. Most of the internet-based companies that disintegrated when the bubble finally burst did so because they simply used this radically new technology to perform existing, run-of-the-mill transactions more efficiently. For Amazon, the ploy never was to use the internet to sell better or more, or just to discount books. It was no less than to change the very way people found, bought and got their books – crafting a new on-line customer experience.

Expedia (once owned by Microsoft and then purchased by Barry Diller's Interactive Corp.) could never have made the impact and captured its customer base of 20 million or so per month, becoming one of the largest on-line travel agents – if not *the* largest – if it had merely sold airline seats with a few extra services welded on to try to differentiate.

Instead, Expedia helps people make their own decisions on where to go; gives them options and choice on how to get there and with whom; provides information on what to do when they get there, depending on whether they are golfers, skiers or adventurers, or whether they want to hit the shows, the shops or the museums; describes how to get around once there; gives suggestions for hotels based on areas, prices and facilities, and organizes bookings for hotels as well as restaurants and theatres; and finally provides useful, even if unasked-for and frequently overlooked, information on the weather and exchange rates at the destination.

It keeps track of customers' plans and continuously updates this data for future trips. It remembers the details distinguishing one customer from another – whether the customer prefers an aisle or a window seat; a vegetarian or a diet meal; the preferred departure, arrival and transfer airports – and it keeps a record of customers' frequent flyer numbers. All of this information is readily available to the Expedia system and easy to pull up whenever necessary, letting Expedia remember all the vital information – so that customers don't have to.

On-line sales aren't only coming from holidaymakers forsaking classic travel agents because they have not been given a fully integrated service: business travellers as well are now making their own reservations, so spending 15 per cent less of their company's time in the process, research shows.[25] This has opened the gap for Expedia to move in with a unified concept to expand a market that didn't even exist just a few years ago, and, in the process, to grow its business while most of its traditional counterparts are left limping behind.

The Integrated Customer Experience

Customer focus means pulling together whatever is needed from various sources across product, service, company and industry lines into one integrated and branded experience. When this is genuinely felt by executives, the implementation is well on its way.

The ramifications are profound: the enterprise, not the customer, does the searching and integrating. The sources may be the various silos inside the enterprise or out, or a combination of both. They may even be competitors.

Customer focus also means finding the best price for customers by aggregating their buying power for their collective benefit, rather than offering discounts to the big transactional purchasers only. If the enterprise can't find that best price in-house, it may, assuming it is one of the more progressive enterprises, look outside, as BP does if it can get a better deal externally for its customers than from its own silos.

Technology makes all of this easier to do today on a mass scale. But technology is not a substitute for the customer-focused approach. Let's stay with BP to demonstrate an example that is more consultative than technological.

In order to energize growth, a series of customer-focused approaches have moved BP away from just the traditional commodity products like gas, oil, bio-thermal power, solar, wind, lubrication and so on. This is because in fact, corporate customers don't care what commodity they use. What they want is to keep their ships, trucks or machines moving (and therefore producing) at the lowest cost and on budget. And since variations in these raw material prices could be between 10 per cent and 40 per cent of their indirect costs, obviously they prefer to keep usage, and hence costs, to the bare minimum. They also increasingly have to worry about the costs associated with environmental damage and liabilities for which they might be held responsible, and from which they can benefit financially if they comply.

Still using BP as an example, the picture changes (from the left of Exhibit 6) from where an enterprise sees itself as a collection of discrete product silos, departments or divisions, to the right side, where it becomes the provider of an integrated experience that leads to a desired outcome for individual customers for which it wants to become indispensable.

Looking at the exhibit, what is significant is that executives see that with true customer focus an enterprise cannot simply be a commodity provider (one of the 'Ps' or providers: see Exhibit 6), because this makes it vulnerable. The exciting opportunity is in the joined-up view of the customer, where the enterprise is able to pull together all of the bits so as to get customer lock-on, accumulate increasing brand power and be in a position to benefit from the profitable revenue streams that ensue.

Once that idea is accepted as a working proposition, the more serious business of making of making it work for a particular enterprise can begin.

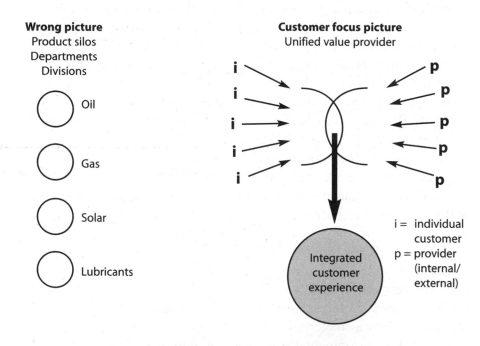

Exhibit 6 Product focus versus customer focus

The Discovery

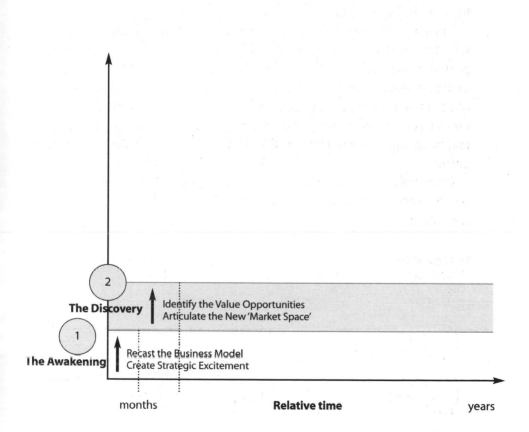

The Discovery ② Identify the Value Opportunities
Articulate the New 'Market Space'

The Awakening ① Recast the Business Model
Create Strategic Excitement

months   **Relative time**   years

Articulate the New Market Space

Broadening Boundaries

A market space definition is vital to achieving the much-needed substance and cohesion at the discovery phase, when people want to start relating the theoretical principles to their own businesses and take the new direction from the abstract to the specific.

This is the time when executives begin to make the all-important decision on where they want to play and how, and so reap the benefits of customer lock-on. Without the market space, which is a descriptive term to frame the new competitive place in which the enterprise wants to flourish, even if the new direction is exciting the organization risks ending up with no more than a checklist of good ideas, inadequate to carry the process on to the next step.

Although executives may know that the new competitive place or competitive arena the enterprise chooses should be outside the limitations of the current set of discrete products and services, they may have difficulty in expressing this in a concrete, meaningful and customer-focused way without a market space definition.

From Chasing Market Share
to
Becoming Indispensable in the Market Space

The market space[26] definition enables executives to move forward, pushing outward, because it frames the extended boundaries to encapsulate the customer outcome, and thus mirrors the unified view of customers in the new way of doing things (see Table 3.1 for examples).

In contrast to obtaining mere market share in product and service categories with their deteriorating benefits, being indispensable in

Table 3.1 Market space examples

Product/service	Market space
BP	
Oil, wind, solar power, gas, bio-thermal energy	'Integrated energy and environmental management'
GE Finance	'Employee mobility assurance'
Fleet financing	
International Health Insurance (IHI)	'Lifetime health and personal safety management'
Health insurance	
(Division) Lexis Nexis	'High-level decision support'
Publishing content	
Webstar Healthcare	'Enhanced medicine performance'
Pharmaceutical dispensing	

delivering the outcome to customers in this market space with all the consequent gains – competitive and financial – becomes the driving force for the transforming enterprise or a newcomer seeking to disrupt the way an industry operates.

Looking at the table, we see this potentially happening in all the examples. Take Webstar Healthcare, a newcomer: for decades already, dispensing had become a commodity in the UK and elsewhere. 'Pharmacists had been saying we are at the crossroads, something drastic is needed if we are to survive. But, conservative by nature, they didn't know what to do and so did nothing.'

Musa Dhalla and his partner Gianpiero Celino decided to do something about it in the year 2000. They left their careers in pharmaceutical wholesaling and started a new UK-based venture whose goal was to shift pharmacists away from simply dispensing medicine by filling prescriptions, to instead becoming more involved in the 'enhanced medicine performance' market space.

The idea was simple: Webstar Healthcare would become indispensable (no pun intended) to pharmacists by helping them to help ordinary people get the best out of the medicine they were prescribed, rather than simply being a channel for getting drugs to patients. Webstar Healthcare's initiative was to design and deliver the systems that linked and brought together pharmacists with drug manufacturers, patients and those who paid for the medication.

In this market space, the partners believed, lay the opportunity for pharmacists who knew their patients' profiles, disposition and history better than anyone else. Such pharmacists could take on a much more meaningful role by advising, monitoring compliance, re-ordering, preventing or countering side-effects, providing substitutes and so forth, with the end result being a better outcome for patients, hospitals, the healthcare system and the performance of the medicine itself.

Two years after Webstar's founding, major government reforms of the pharmaceutical sector in the UK, and happening at different speeds across the world, gave the two entrepreneurs the added impetus they needed to take their growing brand and reputation still further. Now the law would give pharmacists more supplementary prescribing power and allow them to become more involved with other non-dispensing activities. They would also be able to participate in deciding on the best way of treating a patient and changing dosages once the treatment had begun. Under certain conditions, they would even be able to prescribe drugs themselves. For instance, emergency hormonal contraception – the 'morning after' pill – was something pharmacists could now decide to supply without needing a prescription from a hospital or doctor, as was the case before.

Making Connections

Getting executives to make the connection between market spaces and the future of the enterprise, and how this future will be different from the past, is probably the most significant breakthrough of all. This is because the market space not only becomes the new core purpose of the enterprise, but also the red thread holding people and process together as the transformation progresses.

Also when the market space is articulated, an enterprise-wide picture emerges, enabling people across different product silos and disciplines to visualize how they fit into a new joined-up customer concept.

For example, employees at Lexis Nexis used to consider themselves as working in one of the umpteen databases – or units – within the company, but there was no market underpinning to unite them, or the offerings, to ensure superior and quicker customer decisions. However, once top management broadened boundaries to reflect the customer outcome, namely 'high-level decision support', and this was articulated as the market space in which the Corporate and Federal Division of Lexis Nexis was going to play and excel, employees gained clarity, direction and a common sense of purpose, all of which pushed the process along each step of the way.

Words are Important

The words used to express the market space are important. GE Finance in Europe, a division of GE Capital, demonstrates this. Here 'employee mobility assurance' means 'we will take responsibility to get your employees where they need to go', which is significantly different and has very different implications from a definition like 'mobility management'; that is more about doing things to help in the process of getting employees to and from their destination.

In the BP energy example, the word 'integrated' implies that any form of energy will be included as part of the offering, not either oil or solar or gas. If BP wants to deliver an integrated energy customer concept, it needs to acknowledge that to produce such an outcome it would have to make that its (core) business, to know what form of energy is best for each customer and supply and deliver it across business units.

The words used in a market space definition can mean the difference between experiencing a breakthrough during the discovery phase – driving the customer focus process forward because people begin to feel they're on right track – or its having the reverse effect and winding down interest and energy.

As a guideline, a good market space will:

- focus on a desired or unimagined outcome for customers
- be instantly understood and recognized as relevant with potential for growth
- be imaginative, novel and forward looking
- make people excited, compelling them to want to move ahead
- evoke curiosity, opening up windows for dialogue on meaning, relevance and implications.

Deciding on the Market Space

The market space, because it gives concrete shape and form to the otherwise conceptual idea of a unified customer concept, is vital to moving people along the customer focus process. It also stirs and excites them because they begin to feel that they now have something tangible to say about the new direction and what they can do to help steer the enterprise forward.

Once the decision on what market space to choose has been taken, another important breakthrough has been made. It acts as a guide to resolving the oft-pressing question: 'How far do we go?' This sets the parameters for both what must be done to obtain the outcome, and what would take the enterprise too far beyond its newly extended boundary. So, as one executive put it: 'Go as far as you dare, but then … don't break the rubber band.'

Capturing New Wealth

Just because market spaces define new boundaries doesn't mean that they have to be confining: they can be as creative as the enterprise desires. Lego, for instance, made the leap from building construction toys to the 'family edu-tainment' market space, so providing learning through play, merging fun and education to produce a brand that is strong not merely with kids, but also with people who have kids, and even with 'the child within people'.

Regardless of how ambitious the market space may or may not be, the object is still to make it contained enough to provide definition without being constrained.

From one CEO of a well-known global corporation came this remark, as he got his executive team geared up for the exercise: 'An enterprise shouldn't have more than 5–10 per cent market share in their new market space. If they do, they've defined it too narrowly and there won't be enough room for sustained growth.'

This may prove to be too ambitious for some. However, one powerful motivator for extending boundaries outward is that, once they have been awakened and a unified customer perspective has been accepted, executives are often amazed to find out how little the wealth they have been getting in the market space, compared to that gained by other players. For instance, pharmaceutical manufacturers are still only capturing around 10 per cent of the total spend in the lifetime wellbeing market space.[27] This includes alternative remedies, which can be substantial, bearing in mind that in the United States close to half the population is prepared to fork out money from their own pocket for alternative remedies; a trend likely soon to be mirrored in many other parts of the world.

Decisions on market space are often based 'more on the spirit and sights of an enterprise' than on its size or industry. 'It's about foresight and the ability to see where the action is likely to be, and then taking the steps to make sure that you're in first, fast and feisty.'

In reality, executives tend to balance potential with passion. If the potential is there but they feel it's too big to tackle, they will scale down; if they feel strongly enough, they will find a way to make it happen.

Market Space Constructs

Constructs help in the decision-making process.

CONSTRUCT 1: EXISTING – EMERGING – IMAGINED

Market spaces go into one of three categories, progressing from existing to emerging and then to imagined. Depicting them in this way provides a context to help people make a choice on what is appropriate for the organization.

As the transforming enterprise moves from the existing to the emerging and then the imagined market space, the outcome required becomes more sophisticated and requires more complexity. But it also opens up more room for customer lock-on and new wealth, and closes still more doors still more tightly to competitors.

Let's go back to healthcare to illustrate:

Existing market space
Diagnose and prescribe   'disease management'

Emerging market space
Predict, reverse, prevent   'managed healthcare'

Imagined market space
Prolong, preserve 'extended life and wellbeing'

In the existing market space, namely 'disease management', the assumption is that a patient already has, say, cardiac disease and the desirable outcome would be to get it diagnosed accurately and quickly and managed with minimum pain and discomfort, maximizing and accelerating healing, and trying to hold off or reduce the risk of recurrence.

In the 'managed healthcare' market space, the assumption is that patients do not have the disease but that if they're predisposed, they would be told or shown how to detect early warning signals; that these would be spotted with advanced technology before the onset of the disease; that individuals would be helped to prevent the disease and, if it happened nonetheless, to reverse its progress and staunch its side effects, minimize damage if caught quickly enough, speed up healing, and prevent recurrence.

In the 'extended life and wellbeing' market space the assumption is that the patient may never get the disease. Prenatal intervention could be used with the help of genetics to assess whether predispositions to certain diseases exist; then the necessary precautions would be taken to prevent or delay the onset, preserve potentially affected organs, even develop alternative organs if a transplant may be needed in the future, and do whatever else is necessary to make sure that the disease never manifests; or, if and when it does, to minimize the threat to the individual's life and lifestyle.

Venturing into the imagined space does not preclude an enterprise from also being in the emerging and existing market spaces for different markets or countries.

Take GE Fleet Services: from fleet financing, a commodity for all intents and purposes, its market spaces became:

Existing market space 'fleet financial management' – for customers who still want to own the cars and are looking for advice on financing options and funding.

Emerging market space 'vehicle fleet management', which encompasses much more – it presupposes that vehicles need to be sourced, leased and managed throughout their lifespan, and then sold or traded in for new vehicles. Additionally, fuel usage is monitored; insurance and driver training supplied; maintenance, history and accident reports collected; on-line invoicing provided, as well as cost and management reporting that allows fleet managers to reconcile bills easily and do their forecasts to keep getting a better outcome.

Imagined market space – the outcome here is 'employee mobility assurance' for those companies that do not want to own or for that matter lease vehicles. The object is to make cars available to employees when, where and how they need them. It would entail knowing the movement of employees, say technicians for a software company, moving around as they do in order to fix and maintain systems year in and year out. What cars do the technicians need, where and when? What tools do they need inside these cars? What airports do they need to get to and back from? What's the best route to take to get to their customers? What's the closest gas station for them to fill up at? How much gas do they use and what's their energy efficiency? What preventive maintenance would minimize the risk of delays along the way and what back-up is required in the event of a breakdown?

CONSTRUCT 2: SPACES AND SUBSPACES

Construct 2 works with the same principle as for the first, except that the configuration breaks down into subspaces and sub-subspaces depending on the complexity and potential. Often enterprises start in a more contained subspace and then progress over time from this subspace to larger spaces.

Take Amazon: it began with one overriding aim, to become the world's largest bookstore in a market space – call it 'enhanced book buying'. It changed the customer's experience by personalization and contact, helping customers progress from fairly ill-defined needs to discover what they were really after, even if they didn't know what it was exactly. It used various techniques to achieve this, including matching individual profiles to products, and offering authoritative views and alternative suggestions.

Now Amazon is entering a larger space, namely 'knowledge management'. Instead of individuals having to buy books sight unseen, they can virtually flip through the pages and indexes of several books, looking for specific words or phrases, searching and rounding up the information they need for a project – say a speech, essay, report, presentation – or for their own interest and personal development.

Throughout, Amazon's primary aim has been to get to know customers better than anyone else, and it is this that has not only given it a form of customer lock-on never before imagined possible, but also enabled it to evolve into a virtual mall. Now Bezos intends to have the largest selection of goods on earth, obviously in a much wider market space.

IBM is another example of this natural progression from subspace to larger spaces. Louis Gerstner resurrected IBM by getting it from making and selling boxes, its erstwhile occupation, to achieving customer focus through services to help users buy, integrate and run their computers and software in the 'information technology (IT) systems management' market space. As technology advanced, however, 'networking capability' became the important outcome, and 'information technology systems management' was merely one part of it to help customers link and manage the networks they needed within and without the company to compete across the globe (see Exhibit 7).

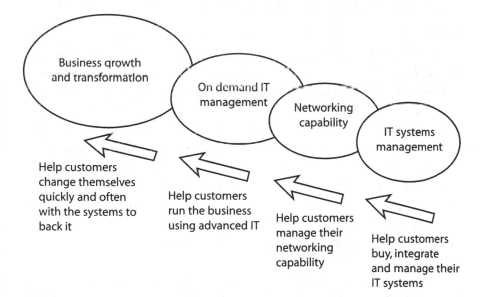

Exhibit 7 Market spaces and subspaces: IBM

New CEO Sam Palmisano has rejuvenated the enterprise yet again, and the next leap has taken it into a larger market space, namely 'on-demand computing'.[28] Like any utility model, corporate customers are now provided with computing power by IBM based on when, where, how and how much (variable) they need. This increases customers' ability to improve marketing planning procurement and customer service processes productivity amongst others, increasing their productivity while also decreasing their costs.

Pushing still further, Palmisano and his team bought the management consultancy arm of PricewaterhouseCoopers, and merged IBM's hardware software, IT consulting unit and about 3000 research scientists with it. Moving well beyond just making computers and programs to run them better quicker, the aim was direct entry into the higher ground 'business growth and transformation' market space. Through the use of sophisticated technologies using multiple forms of data and research techniques, the object here is to extract, extrapolate and expose trends to give executives unique insights into fast-moving marketplace opportunities that they can capture, as well as the technological systems they need to get there.[29]

Some enterprises, like IBM or Amazon, will naturally gravitate into the larger market spaces 'because that's where the action is'. Others will be more cautious, playing in the smaller subspaces to be closer to what they feel they know.

Irrespective of that, as long as a market space has been articulated, understood and enthusiastically accepted, everything else follows.

Identify the Value Opportunities

Value Gaps and Black Holes

The market space tells an enterprise where to aim in a competitive place, framing the new ways of doing things as a customer outcome. It is thus fundamental to creating a customer focused organization.

The question that follows is: what value components are needed to ensure a customer experience that produces that outcome?

Using the customer activity cycle executives can obtain very specific answers to this question, because it is a structured methodology that looks at the activities that customers go, or could or should go, through to get an outcome, then uncovers the gaps or shortfalls, and fills these gaps with the missing value components.[30]

Why Gaps Destroy Value

Specifically, the value gaps to be found in a customer activity cycle are:

- things not being done for customers during an experience
- things being done badly for the customer during an experience
- things being done by customers themselves that could be done either better or cheaper by the provider.

When these gaps exist, they create disconnects that interfere with the customer's experience and prevent the outcome – desired or unimagined by customers – being achieved, thus destroying rather than creating value. That is when, as we have seen, companies or industries fall, even the biggest and best.

This is because these value gaps effectively become gaping black holes into which the enterprise gradually slides or implodes, depending on how quickly others – usually outsiders – enter to create the value and consequently steal their customers and the existing or potential new revenue streams.

When value gaps happen everyone can lose, including customers. The consequences to them range from disenchantment to discomfort, serious loss of time, money, effort or, something even more serious, increased costs in the short or long terms.

Customers may not be aware of this loss or increased cost until a new innovative approach is offered and its benefits revealed. Then they move elsewhere when a disruptor who appears on the scene offers that alternative.

For instance, a not-so-well-known fact is that about a quarter of all relocations fail.[31] Executives may also be late in starting their assignments in the new country or unproductive once there. These are hidden costs that do not appear on any specific budget. Their occurrence can be largely due to the fact that the executives, or their spouses or children, are unhappy or unsuited to the climate or culture of the country to which they have been expatriated. These costs, research shows, can mount up to nearly £1 million per posting over a three-year assignment.[32]

What is relevant here is that the problem starts with a value gap: most of the relocation decisions taken about whom to send where are based on the skills of an individual, rather than also on consideration of the family profile and levels of comfort. Matching people more accurately to environments obviates this.

Other gaps occur once professionals are in the foreign country. For example, they may need a certain drug and not be able to find it so a poor or no substitute is taken, or the decision about which hospital to go to when something goes wrong is not optimal. Both of these can lead to costly and even devastating ramifications.

Or take a situation where employees are not briefed about corruption and bribery in a particular country to which they have been relocated, and, once ensconced there, are ordered to give business to someone against their will – with a threat that if they don't, their family will suffer. The upshot can be that the person is fearful and acquiesces, leading to deteriorating health and productivity consequences.

Opening Up Opportunities for Killer Entrants

Whole industries can be built up around value gaps left unfilled in market spaces left undefined. We only have to think back to IBM in the old days to illustrate the point. While IBM was selling mainframes and PCs, customers needed consulting advice, software integration and so on. They wanted procurement advice and help with purchasing (as opposed to selling), pilot testing, integration and a whole lot else, as well as proactive remote and preventive maintenance and speedy responses to problems that IBM didn't give – but third parties did. All of this added value became the new wealth that went to newcomers.

We all know that this is now history, but the tale is worth repeating nonetheless, because similar events keep on happening on a grand scale. Look at the airline business – no-frill disruptors entered its market space, simply eliminating the gaps such as poor food, badly equipped airports, ticketing structures and the like, which customers were paying for and either didn't think worked, or didn't want, or didn't value.

Once competitors find these value gap windows, they become killer entrants, quickly jump in and provide the fully unified customer outcome or, having found an entry point, build a reputation, relationships, vital links and trust with the customer base. They are then able to move around the customer's activity cycle gradually, in the process broadening and absorbing customer spend.

Direct Line is a good example. Having captivated and captured customers by helping them get and manage their insurance differently, it moved to actually offering advice on cars, financing, and then into breakdown and emergency services, for which it is now the largest provider in the UK, superseding legends the Royal Automobile Club (RAC) and the Automobile Association (AA), both of which have remained primarily focused only on the emergency services.

The Customer Activity Cycle Methodology

The customer activity cycle model has three stages (see Exhibit 8):

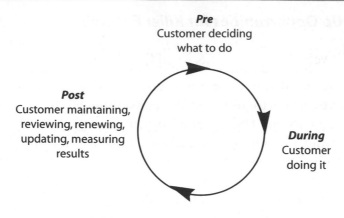

Exhibit 8 Generic customer activity cycle

Pre: when the customer is deciding what to do

During: when the customer is doing it

Post: when the customer is maintaining, reviewing, renew-
            ing, updating and measuring the results of what he or
            she decided to do.

The customer activity cycle technology uncovers details of activities
customers go through *pre*, *during* and *post* an experience, exposing
what is preventing the outcome at each critical point and then speci-
fying exactly what is needed at each of these critical points to get the
outcome, such as 'high-level decision support' to make critical decisions better and more quickly; or 'lifelong health and personal safety'
to ensure expatriate wellbeing rather than merely buy health insurance
policies.

Abstract ideas can thus become tangible enough to advance the
implementation further.

To return to a previous example, the country manager at Baxter
Germany might have discovered a new market space. But it was only
when the customer activity cycle revealed what needed to be done *pre*
treatment, *during* treatment and *post* treatment to get a better outcome
for patients at home, as well as for doctors and for hospitals, that
executives could be concrete about the values that would need to be

delivered, and by whom, to be able to negotiate both inside the enterprise and with potential partners. This led to the ultimate formation of the new joint venture, Home Supply and Care (HSC).

Getting In Sooner

To lock on customers and lock out competition, the object is to get into the customer's activity cycle as early as possible – and to stay in longer.

Pre is when customers make decisions on what to do. The potential to influence (not just promote) and build integrity (not just hard sell) is therefore at its peak. This could mean matching profiles to product, which may even be a competitor's product – nearly half of the hard(er)ware that IBM sells is not its own.

When there are value gaps at this *pre* stage, the chances are that the customers may make the wrong decision, which may prevent the desired outcome from taking place. That is why International Health Insurance's emphasis is on preventive interventions as early as possible, before an illness happens.

Not being present at the *pre* stage will certainly diminish the chances of the enterprise influencing and solidifying its position with customers when it matters. The incredible impetus harnessed by independent consultants in the last few decades is due to that lack of presence by suppliers, which not merely pulled their customer power away, but also lost them revenues, as the consultants moved around the activity cycle to influence their mainstream and take new potential business.

As to how early interventions should occur, the guideline is: the earlier the better. Lexis Nexis could simply wait for customers to ask questions and then find them the information they are after. But instead, the power of its new proposition is that it prompts customers to ask the correct questions so they themselves can take the correct decisions. For example, one way law enforcement agencies may locate criminals or the drugs or other undesirable or illegal items they store is by asking the question: who has taken out a pilot's or driver's licence in that area recently?

Importantly, each of these layers of questions and answers moves seamlessly into the others, so they fit into the customers' daily work pattern without their having to stop working to do that research.

Enterprises that have no presence at the *pre* stage in their market space become vulnerable to third parties. For instance, rather than wait for a specification on a new system from the administrative work that oozes out when doctors, hospitals, reimbursers, local service providers (LSPs) and government are linked to enhance the performance of medicine, Webstar Healthcare gets involved in the design of the system early on, and even gives free advice on what system will work the best and the most cost-efficiently.

In B2B settings, opportunities emerge early on for dealing in the boardroom and with senior management when decisions are taken about new directions and strategies that influence what customers buy and from whom. That kind of thinking prompted Hewlett-Packard to make a bid (ultimately unsuccessful) to buy Pricewater-houseCoopers, rather than being left out on a limb to simply wait for hardware orders, which would never have brought it the real growth it wanted. IBM, which later did buy the consulting arm of Price-waterhouseCoopers, moved itself into the higher consulting ground with a view to genuinely helping organizations transform the way they analyse the marketplace and make strategic decisions.

Staying In Longer

In the old days, once the transaction ended, that was that until the next transaction. Then came the services era in the mid-1980s, in which the great learning was that a good deal of the monies spent on a product or service happened after the original sale. The figures were astounding: services post-sale had the potential to exceed first-time sales by 10 to 30 times. Between 10 and 25 per cent of the revenues for, say, cars or computers come from services, which contribute an even greater percentage of the profits.[33]

Then came the bad news. The same battle for market share of *post* services began with the same deteriorating consequences – customers moving around, looking for the best deals – and here too margins began to decrease.

Providing value components *post* is key to customer focus, but it's more than after-sales service. It's also the time when customers are renewing, updating, reviewing and measuring, and ideally, when customer lock-on has been achieved, this is done automatically with the existing supplier – rather than the customer looking to justify the previous decision or revise the original choice of supplier at this crucial time.

Thus it is vital that an enterprise wanting to make it to true customer focus learns how to demonstrate to customers that they are better off with it than without it, based on hard evidence. This ability to measure the outcome becomes part of the core capabilities of the truly customer-focused enterprise.

Creating Customer Value

The breakthrough at this part of process is the discovery that while value gaps left in the customer activity cycle bring about the damage we see so often today, the value components that fill gaps offer the growth opportunities – if only they can be identified and specified.

It is these very discontinuities that give the enterprise the chance to create customer value. These fall into two categories:

Putting value in: these are activities that contribute to getting the outcome, for instance training on corruption and bribery so the employee knows what to do if faced with that situation in a foreign country. Or helping a manufacturer reuse or convert its energy to save on cost and environmental damage. Or compiling a complete universe of information on a real-time basis for lawyers to access while they are building a case.

Taking out non-value: these are activities being done by the customer that eat into time, energy and money without contributing to, or destroying attempts to achieve, an outcome. They can be removed by the transforming enterprise, like warning a person not to rush to the airport if a flight is delayed. Or preventing a lawyer from having to sift through massive quantities of documents – maybe a million or more – and having to hire a roomful of people to do so, while in litigation.

How Disconnects Unlock Value

Jeff Bezos created exactly this kind of value in Amazon's original 'enhanced book buying' market space, which earned the company steady growth and an amassed pool of millions of customers, leaving competitors way behind.

Bezos saw the disconnects, the innumerable opportunities to put value in and the oh-so-many non-value-adding activities that manifested themselves in wasted time, hassles and costs. These included a customer having to get to the bookstore (sometimes several), searching to find a book (they may not even know which one), trying to get assistance, ordering the book if it is not in stock, queuing to pay and, if they are unlucky, having to return and start the process all over again!

In his unified view of the customer, Bezos then set about providing added value at each critical point *pre*, *during* and *post* the customer's experience, to fill both the leisure and professional sides of people's lives.

Because the major thrust was to get to know who people are and what they read, do, like or find useful, insights and suggestions based on the customer's profile enabled Amazon to become a proactive force no matter how diverse customers' interests or preoccupations were, from writing their MBA theses to building a perfect rose garden. Since customers don't always know what kind of book they want or need, Amazon became more than an order taker: it provided lists in categories, acting more like a library, as well as an index and summary of these books, allowing people to flip through them as they would in a bookstore, but much more easily.

By tracking customers who read and do the same things, it made connections between unlikely topics like, say, the role of rose gardens in medieval poetry. Customers are also offered books they never knew existed, including what can be obtained on that subject in DVD, video, and CD-Rom formats.

After an order is placed, so intimate is Amazon's knowledge of the customer that it will alert the person to the fact that he or she may have ordered a duplicate book. Keeping track of what customers have purchased, Amazon also acts as a clearing house, and can value book collections and offer to buy them back and turn them into cash or a credit.

Amazon also works with 'bricks and mortar' retail merchants, large and small, helping them grow the on-line side of their businesses without having to start from scratch or undergo the formidable costs and hassles involved, including making the mistakes that Amazon has learned to avoid. By designing the merchants' websites, and building the appropriate technology platforms, Amazon makes it easy for these merchants' customers to shop – choosing, buying, paying, and getting redress when they have a problem – on-line now, as well as off.

In addition, the smaller, niche-type publishers, music labels and studios that offer items that customers may want but could never find – either because they don't know they exist, or because they can't locate them, since most of these small enterprises don't have websites – are given access to Amazon's huge marketing and distribution machine together with one of the world's largest audiences. This is done at a nominal rate to create a better experience for the customer and to give these small players access they would never otherwise have. If items are sold, Amazon will process the order within 24 hours, ship it anywhere in the world, monitor inventory and automatically send an email request for additional copies based on customer demand.

Using the Customer Activity Cycle Tool

The object of the customer activity cycle is to get executives to unearth the value components that will form the basis of the new innovative customer approach. Here are the questions:

1 What are the critical activities customers go through or could/should go through to get the outcome as defined by the market space?
2 What are the opportunities for intervention and adding value by:
    – putting value in?
    – taking non-value out?

Table 4.1 lists some 'dos' and don'ts' when using the methodology.

Table 4.1 Using the customer activity cycle methodology

Don't:	Do:
work haphazardly	work through *pre*, then *during*, then *post*
fill in value adds at random as people get ideas	first go through the customer activity cycle, look for gaps, then fill in the value components
get sidetracked by what you presently do	concentrate on what you don't presently do: otherwise there is no added value
allow individuals to use their own versions of the methodology	keep the method consistent so experience is transferable to others across the enterprise
use paper, pen and notebooks	use post-its, or work with a PC to allow for instant alterations and improvisations
try to prove anything with data	use people who know the customer, or have an 'educated, intuitive' feel

Finding the Hidden Gold

International Health Insurance (IHI) had two major segments: individuals mostly living abroad for work or play, and corporations with employees at home, travelling or living in foreign countries. Pushing ever outward in both cases, the intriguing challenge in Per Bay Jorgensen's revitalization of the Danish enterprise in 2000 was to discover what value adds would turn the growing awareness that wellness pays – not merely because people feel better, but because it costs less overall.

Exhibit 9 illustrates the simplified IHI customer activity cycle, showing what customers do or could/should do to get a health and personal safety outcome.

IHI is an example of how a string of value adds can be put into the customer activity cycle at each critical point in the customer's experience. When these are connected they attain the desired outcome, in this case 'lifetime personal health and safety management' (see Exhibit 10).

Choosing Where to Aim

Executives may initially decide to focus on only the *pre*, *during* or *post* stage of the customer activity cycle. So long as this represents a full and comprehensive view of the customer outcome, it can be done and made to work.

Take the new Baxter Healthcare HSC initiative in Germany with partners. Patients who are seriously ill go through the three stages in their customer activity cycle: *pre* the operation when they get the symptoms and decide what to do, *during* the operation when they experience the various procedures – medical and other – that accompany this, and *post*, when they are being rehabilitated.

It was clear to all involved at Baxter Germany that there were practical reasons for positioning the new venture in the *post* operation stage of the customer activity cycle. Then the challenges associated with managing the value adds that patients needed outside the conventional hospital setting – inside their homes, giving treatments such as dialysis and chemotherapy, nutrition, pain relief, as well as the provision of drugs like antibiotics and other medication – would be unique.

Lifetime health and personal safety management 'market space'

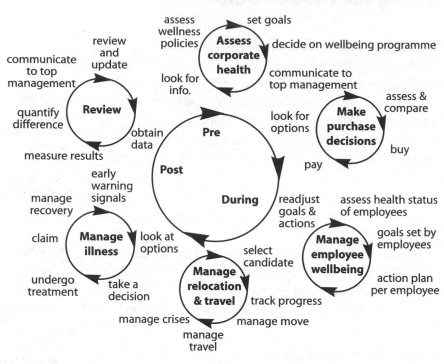

Exhibit 9 International Health Insurance (IHI) corporate customer activity cycle (simplified)

The leap was taken into this *post* operation stage in what we could call the 'home rehabilitation management' market space. Here the enterprise proceeded to track all the activities that customers go through in the old conventional system, and then build a new unified customer experience using the tool to identify each value add at each critical point, so that new ways for customers to recover at home could become real and realized.

When patients leave the hospital *post* operation but *pre* home treatment, typically the physicians will prescribe what is to be done. Before Home Supply and Care (HSC) takes the patient on, however, another *pre* home treatment activity is undertaken (see Exhibit 11). This involves doing home assessments, ostensibly to ascertain the home's suitability to provide the necessary facilities, from layout to water purity. Staff then meet with family and friends, talking through what

Lifetime health and personal safety management 'market space'

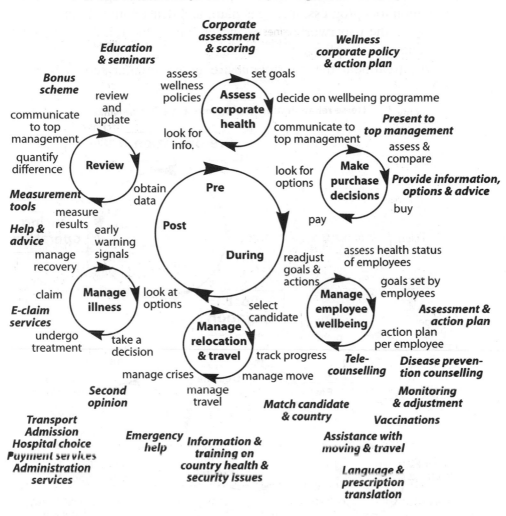

Exhibit 10 IHI corporate customer activity cycle and value adds (simplified)

needs to be done and some of the psychological burdens they can expect in supporting the patient.

After assessment is made and the patient is taken on, HSC gets into the *during* treatment stage, when friends, family and the patient are given counselling and training and the physical conditions are prepared. HSC then sources, orders, delivers and administers the medical and nutritional treatments plus additional drugs and medication, monitors progress, manages pain, and deals with side-effects. It also does the paperwork, makes the claims to the reimbursers, gets paid and pays suppliers.

Post treatment the physicians are given regular feedback and

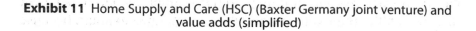

Home rehabilitation management 'market space'

Pre-operation

During operation

Post operation

change stabilize treatment

feedback physician

Post treatment

Pre-treatment

assess treatment home needs

update treatment

assess home facilities e.g. purity of water

assess layout of home

manage side-effects

During treatment

assess family/ friend support

apply treatments

source treatments

counsel family & patient

monitor treatments

buy treatments

layout and install in home

pain management

get reimbursement

pay

deliver treatments & other medications

train patient

do paperwork

Exhibit 11 Home Supply and Care (HSC) (Baxter Germany joint venture) and value adds (simplified)

patients are returned to them if needed for a check-up or for changing or updating the treatment or prescription.

Exhibit 11 shows this in diagrammatic form.

Drilling Down for Opportunities

BP is another example. Providing integrated energy and environmental management to hauliers involves a complex set of activities in the customer activity cycle, *pre*, *during* and *post* journey, to keep trucks going at maximum capacity and lowest cost, while minimizing their wear and tear and damage to the environment.

Pre journey is from the time the order is received, including planning, truck preparation, route maximization, driver selection and briefing.

During journey includes activities such as navigation, refuelling, breakdowns, rest, getting to destination and delivery.

Post journey includes activities such as administration, paperwork, review of performance, truck maintenance and repair, and getting paid.

As is often the case, it was in the details of the customer activity cycle that the lucrative opportunities lay. BP Commercial Transport, the sponsoring business unit, dug deep into the customer activity cycle for its haulier customers in its newly articulated 'integrated energy and environmental management' market space, drilling (so to speak) down into the main cycle and subcycles (Exhibit 12 illustrates this).

One small value add uncovered came from the fact that in the cabin comfort sub-subcycle, while drivers slept they kept the engines running for warmth. BP learned that this 'idling' amounted to 5 per cent of fuel costs; accounted for 20 per cent of nitrogen oxide and other noxious emissions; and inevitably exacerbated overall wear and tear on the vehicle and engine – costs that equalled 10 per cent of overall fuel expenditure. This was an amount considerable enough to turn suppliers on to the need to get hauliers' engines turned off, and to think about ways to ensure driver comfort during sleep without all the added costs!

The point about the driver comfort subcycle shown in the diagram is that drivers must be kept in top condition and trained, so that they can perform. 'What's the use of fighting over a quarter per cent discount on the fuel if the driver puts his foot down too hard because

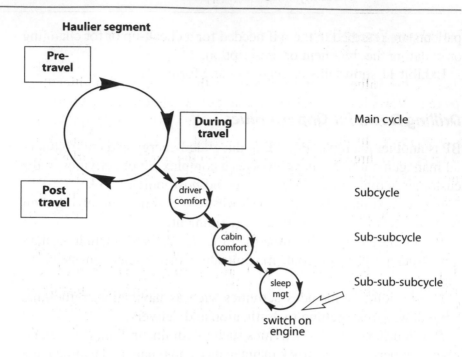

Exhibit 12 BP subcycles (simplified)

he is sitting badly or not sleeping well and so is over-revving and uses five times as much fuel?' In addition, if the journey is made comfortable, a better calibre of person may be attracted to the job, itself a significant challenge for the industry.

Inside this sub-sub-subspace of the haulier customer activity cycle, not only was a value component found to enrich the customer's and employee's experience, but a whole new business opportunity was opened up for BP together with partners.

Getting Traction

Because the value components become the future opportunities that create new wealth for the transforming organization, it's not unusual for this part of the change process to be the most energizing. And it is at this step, in the discovery phase that can take anywhere from two weeks to three months, depending on the number of markets the enterprise decides to work in initially, and the amount of time and resources allocated to the exercise, that executives report feeling the breakthrough and enthusiasm most strongly, and so the customer focus cthos and concepts seriously begin to take grip.

Unless customer focus process gets this traction, first from 'points of light' – the key executives who take the lead – and then from a broader population, an cntcrprise will be stalled in its tracks, unable to implement and move forward. It will constantly be battling with push-back that will dissipate rather than ignite the energy needed to move forward.

The discovery period plays an important part in achieving this traction. First, it allows people to make the all-important decisions about where the enterprise is to play, and frame this in a way that can be inspiring as well as concrete. This brings the customer approach into sharper focus.

Then, because the customer activity cycle tool is a structured methodology, it provides the discipline to keep executives on the customer track. There is also sufficient rigour in the technology to instil them with the confidence to come up with very clear tangible suggestions on how gaps in the customers' experience can be translated into specific customer values.

This becomes all important given that the new direction is often quite abstract and thus difficult for most to grasp at the outset.

The structured approach is nonetheless balanced by an equal dose of creative thinking, because the tool also stimulates people's imagination so they can look for, and find, the not-so-obvious gaps and opportunities. They are also enabled to explore and uncover collectively with colleagues 'what they know, or don't even know they know' and, equally important, discover 'what they don't know about customers and didn't know they didn't know, and need to find out'.

Additionally, according to executives familiar with the technology, the customer activity cycle gets this traction in other ways, including those listed in Box 4.1.

Legitimizing the Team

By this stage, a small team or teams will have been formed, led by collaborating and sponsoring executives with their carefully chosen representatives. Use 'the best brains you've got, not the people you can spare', executives warn over and over again.

Without a team or teams, purposefully constructed, with a clearly defined mission, fully legitimized by this stage, the risk can be miserable failure. This applies especially (but not only) in complex

---

Box 4.1 How the customer activity cycle gets traction

Cementing a common customer theme: 'We felt we were describing the same thing.'

Engaging people: they can contribute even if they are not in contact with customers on a daily basis.

Using it as an organizing tool: it provides a template for a unified view of the customer.

Providing a company-wide view: binding people from different parts of the company because they can now see how and where they fit.

Helping people express conceptual ideas in a tangible way: it allows executives to verbalize what they may have felt but couldn't easily express without a framework.

Being neutral and non-threatening: the new focus enables people who have different and sometimes opposing agenda, to work positively together and jointly explore common ground.

As a powerful communication device: the image is vivid, making it compelling and easy to communicate within and without the organization.

Being robust and structured: it raises people's confidence.

organizations, because people will invariably drift back into their own parts of the organization, start working on various disparate projects unconnected to the main customer theme or each other, and the alignment and momentum gained will be irrevocably lost.

People will probably have been working either full-time or part-time on the exercises so far, but once the customer activity cycle takes off, it is necessary for a specific small core team – around two to five people, again depending on circumstances – to be formed to do the detailed analysis and be permanently involved. 'It's only when the work changed to a day rather than a night job that we began to really make things happen.'

Meetings in small groups will mushroom as this core group scatters to find the collective knowledge they have inside and outside the organization, do the supplementary work and test their ideas, bringing people in when and where needed, and communicating their findings to the wider sponsoring group and audience necessary to pull the process along and draw still others in.

In some enterprises this team – who ideally will be reporting directly to or led by the CEO or sponsoring senior executive – is ringfenced, kept away from the day-to-day operations, able to function within a different set of rules. The object is to shelter it from the restrictions that normally hamper progress, like convoluted procedures and needing consensus to make a decision; although in larger organizations it may still be subject to stage-gates when 'go' or 'no go' decisions are made.

Being ringfenced could also entail being given a set of customers to deal with, to whom the team has exclusive access for a period; using different time horizons or performance criteria; having guaranteed access to people inside the organization but outside the norm; improvising and being allocated resources without presentation of a formal plan.

Signs that Traction is Taking Hold

If traction is consciously managed along the milestones this results in 'stickiness' and people begin to talk with more authority and conviction. Concepts and language are bedded down and start to become 'a code or shorthand' at meetings and during discussions that no one questions any more. Executives claim this is one of the strong signs 'that customer focus has finally taken firm root'.

Some of the other signs that this is happening include:

- more people volunteering to take part in discussions
- more questions about what is happening from all parts of the organization
- active participation and experimentation
- talking with customers to get their informal feedback
- customers and media beginning to ask questions.

Warnings of Distraction

The opposite of the traction that keeps things moving forward is the distraction that pulls people in other directions, slows down the pace and even fizzles or freezes the process out.

Here are the top offenders:

- an unexpected change in business conditions that frightens the powers that be, who postpone initiatives
- disconnects between initiatives in different parts of the organization without commitment to an overarching customer concept or systematic process
- bringing in different outside consultants who pull in different directions
- a sudden decision to prioritize something else that is considered new and hot.

These distractions are usually avoided 'when leaders have faith in themselves and what they are doing' and single-mindedly push ahead with passion and conviction that they deliberately make contagious to those around them.

It takes a combination of courage, patience and, add executives, 'time – more than you think'. All of this is hard to achieve but impossible to do without. This attitude represents what you get from the kind of leader that takes an organization from where it is to where it needs to go in order to make a groundbreaking difference – the time when leadership really matters.

The Story

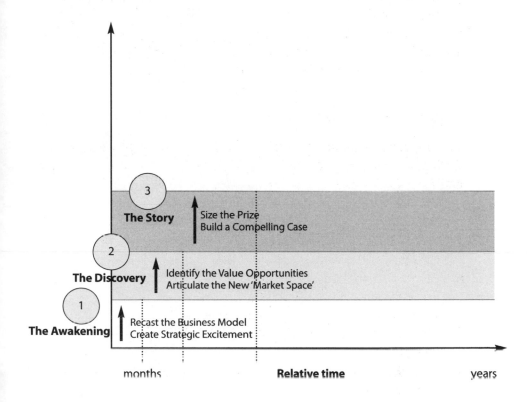

3

The Story ↑ Size the Prize
Build a Compelling Case

2

The Discovery ↑ Identify the Value Opportunities
Articulate the New 'Market Space'

1

The Awakening ↑ Recast the Business Model
Create Strategic Excitement

months   **Relative time**   years

Build a Compelling Case

Stories Versus Business Plans

Storytelling is a vital tool for serious transformations, whether the reconstruction is a gradual reshaping or a revved-up revival; whether it comes in response to an institutional decline or as part of a continuous attempt to harness new opportunities.

Imbued with much more vigour and power than conventional business plans, stories help enterprises build a compelling case so that they can move up and along the change process and make customer focus happen.

People invariably react negatively to business plans, finding them rigid, deadly boring and generally unwelcome: an annual chore, more a control mechanism than a motivator. By contrast, stories are narratives and, if well told and credible, can present an exciting picture that people can identify with and respond to positively.

An old proverb goes, 'Give people a fact or idea and you enlighten their minds: tell them a story and you touch their souls.'[34] Research confirms this ancient wisdom: people actually think in stories. Traditional business plans instruct people, whereas a story engages them emotionally and involves them, as these quotes from executives illustrate:

It's the connection between what we have now and the future.

You identify with it personally and you feel implicated.

You want to know how it will progress.

It compares what you have got to what's possible to get, and that makes you think about what's got to be done and what you have to do.

People believe in stories – they are ingrained in us from birth.

Why Stories are Better

There are many good reasons that stories are better than business plans.

Written with the existing scripted framework in mind, by their very nature traditional business plans work in rigid product terms. So people continue to be mentally programmed to think, talk and behave in this mould and so perpetuate it.

Business plans are built to get people to conform, restricting rather than stretching the imagination. And since they do invariably hold people back, what comes out 'is the same-old same-old, year after year, and before long, it's too late'.

Executives are beginning to realize the limitations of business plans:

Business plans tend to be repetitious from one year to the next – in fact, top management often insists upon that, and the only real change is in the figures.

Table 5.1 Business plans and stories

Traditional business plans describe:	Stories describe:
how to improve what exists	what is going to be done differently
the series of tasks that have to be undertaken	the flow of critical events to be accomplished
an inalterable fixed contract, cast in concrete	how the growth and development will will take place
in one-dimensional terms what each silo is contracted to deliver	a multidimensional view of what's to be achieved, embracing the whole enterprise
separate agendas from different parts of the organization	a unified theme and who fits where
comparisons between different competing parts of the business	collaborative opportunities for working together
hoped-for projections	the possibilities and challenges needed to attain success

They don't make a lasting impact therefore, whereas stories can, and do.

In business plans people write what's predictable and is expected of them, usually the good news, the 'hoped-for projections', instead of looking for what's unpredictable and unexpected and the challenges associated with getting there, which requires a fundamental shift. So the enterprise stays in its product mould instead of breaking out into uncharted territory and looking for something unique and different.

Traditional business plans are a snapshot of what is to be achieved in a very short space of time in the year ahead. In contrast, there is a natural flow to a story: it emerges as the milestones pass by, which happens over time when a degree of improvisation and experimentation is allowed in order to get to the innovative end state and build a platform for continued success.

When Business Plans are Budgets

Perhaps the biggest handicap to using traditional business plans is that they are more like contracts and budgets than descriptions of how a company is going to reconstruct or refresh itself.

They are more like a contract to produce the financials we all know we may never achieve in any case.

Business plans just show the numbers; it's the columns with the figures and the calculations people want to see, not what we want to do.

The numbers in a business plan may also not be feasible, so any unexpected change can render them instantly null and void. Forecasts not met then have an impact on share prices, morale and credibility, with all the ripple effects.

So the most important problem is that business plans reinforce silo mentalities, preventing any unified view of the customer from emerging. Unlike stories, which present a multidimensional perspective that embraces the whole enterprise, business plans are typically just a set of discrete agendas from different parts of the organization aggregated up. Often the bits are unrelated and have no real story to tell about a future the enterprise will be part of or is trying to create. The business plan says 'nothing inspiring about where the company is going or what it has to do to get there, or why people should become interested or engaged in the first place'.

When and how budgets and financial goals are going to be achieved is a part of the organization's story, but only a part: 'You never get rid of the figures. But if new initiatives end up just as business plans which are nothing more than contracts or budgets based on products, customer focus will never happen.'

Stories are Told

To make a case powerfully so that people react and act accordingly, a story must be communicated in a compelling way. Its structure and presentation are therefore as important as its content or message.

'You *tell* a story' – it's a description of something that can happen if actions are taken. Stories are aimed at getting people's attention and making them interested because they become engaged on both the emotional and rational levels. As one expert commentator on the subject put it: 'At the most basic level, storytelling can help a manager gain and hold his audience's attention. But if the story is good enough, it can also lift individuals and organizations to take the risks that keep life an adventure.'[35]

The point is that if people want to excite and enthuse others to make fundamental changes that become a way of life, embedded into the corporate fabric for all time, they have to get them to *feel* something rather than just *telling* them something. Most business plans don't do that. 'They show the data in the hope that someone will read it and study it, and you pray that it happens as you said it would.' 'Instead, the passion must come through and that can never happen in the kinds of documents and modus operandi that have been used in the past.'

When Gerstner arrived at IBM as the new CEO, he found that the company was being 'managed by foils'. An executive would come to a meeting, present these foils or overhead slide presentations, then ask for funds and either get them or not, depending on how the numbers looked. Although the newly appointed CEO did ask for written proposals in advance, the time he spent with executives went into discussing and interrogating. It is said that on at least one occasion he walked into a conference room and ripped out the projector's power cord! [36]

What is also to be avoided is constructing a story and then presenting it in conventional corporate speak and format. The old formula and new ideas and concepts won't fit together and executives won't get the reactions that matter from people, even though the elements for customer focus may be present. In addition, too much detail initially can be a disadvantage. As one executive said: 'If you get swamped down in too much detail at the beginning you just can't move; the object should be to give as much as is necessary but use it to get out and show that it can work.'

Building the Story Around Customers

A product consisting of computing grids that can pool the collective data processing and storage capabilities of large networks with machines that diagnose and self-repair to avoid services being disrupted – what all of this takes and costs in R&D patents and investment is impressive. Having scientists, computer specialists and systems analysts, mathematicians, anthropologists and sociologists working together to look at how technology can help decision making in a way that experts have never done before is an intriguing prospect.

However, what is important is to get people to imagine and aspire to a world that they are in the midst of creating, in which a corporate customer will be at the forefront of breakthrough ideas through research and expertise, able to analyse markets and make decisions that put it out front, influencing the organization at the highest possible level. And people will have computing systems that arrive on demand, like a tap delivers water or a switch creates light, in order to deliver those ideas into the market and run their businesses more effectively.

This is the story that IBM now tells as it tackles the next round in its quest to grow through customers – a story not about the next big technology, but about how it will work for customers.

Part of that story was the acquisition of PricewaterhouseCoopers' consulting arm. This was not merely a move to do more of the same, but rather a move to combine the talents of two organizations, neither of which could on its own accomplish what customers really needed – a technology relevant to their specific business practice.

For an enterprise to implement customer focus seriously – whether it's the first time round or another cycle in its ongoing rejuvenation, as is the case with IBM – the core team must build a story for its various audiences around how customers will benefit. These audiences – the board, top management, peers, partners or investors – will be the ones to act as filters, feeders and funders along the way, determining how far the enterprise reaches and how fast the process progresses if it is to reach its ultimate potential.

Ultimately this will be the story of the new organization the team wants customers to lock on to, rather than having them simply respond to an announcement of more new, often disparate, products and services that make the old ones obsolete and, in retrospect, may not be such a good investment after all.

All the activities that have gone before – dispelling beliefs that can irrevocably hurt an enterprise or cause it to miss out on opportunities irrespective of how well it may or may not be doing; exposing people to new concepts to align thinking and decision making outwards to customers; defining the market space to frame the customer outcome; mapping the customer activity cycle to identify the customer value adds to achieve this outcome – are all preludes to building this next breakthrough in the process of making customer focus happen. What is required is a story built around customers that intrigues people and motivates them to want to participate and thus push the process forward that next, crucial step.

Beginning with the New Core Purpose

Generally when a conventional approach is used the organization begins with a mission statement, which often says little that is very different from what others are saying. The concept of market spaces has two specific advantages at the front end, when a good story is introduced around customers.

First, it articulates the new broadened boundary and aspirations for the enterprise compared with the status quo. Second, from there it quite naturally translates this into the new core purpose, representing a set of sentiments and commitments, the centre of gravity binding the enterprise to new ways of doing things for customers.

To International Health Insurance, for instance, taking the enterprise into the 'lifetime health and personal safety management' market space would mean a new core purpose that embodied:

Lifetime:

- Helping people take decisions on prevention and intervention, which can have a significant impact on their lifelong wellbeing, not simply pay claims when they fall ill.
- Including post retirement, a time when health insurance becomes imperative but also exceedingly expensive, and people often find

they have no protection because enterprises generally only cover them for as long as they remain on the payroll.

Health:

- Maximizing the individual's chances of staying well and in top form ('healthier people are more productive, happier, and less costly'), by understanding the health risk factors.
- Doing what's needed to assist in preserving the health of individuals or employees working for other parties.

Personal safety:

- Including the personal safety of independent customers or employees travelling or living in foreign lands.
- Avoiding the many minor and major things that could go wrong, with all the ensuing problems and costs.

Management:

- Being there for customers (virtually and physically), getting them to the best service and treatment available for their specific needs irrespective of their or their providers' locations.
- Assisting them through the various systems or procedures to save time and hassles. And measuring results to further foster and nurture relationships for life.

The Backbone of the Story

When the customer activity cycle is used as an organizing tool to build and communicate stories, the stories can be visually as well as intellectually compelling. It's the best way to use the analysis, package it in a message and get people to see what needs to be done and how. The customer activity cycle communicates the specifics of how the core purpose will be translated into the offering portfolio.

The customer values that connect to form the outcome become the building blocks of the storyline. They are also the backbone to the new set of offerings beginning at the *pre* stage, when customers are making decisions about how to get an outcome, and ending *post*, when they are reviewing their decisions to determine whether or not to go back into the loop and with whom.

Going back to IHI, its customer value repertoire echoed its intent to become intimately involved with customer wellness and not simply sell policies or process claims for illness expenses (see Exhibit 13).

In a story spanning a multitude of values, the small innovation team working with the CEO built a case around the critical points in the customer activity cycle and the values they had uncovered that translated into an offering portfolio that would lead to wellbeing. This was based on the fact that diseases and disorders can be prevented 70 per cent of the time and that, because problems can

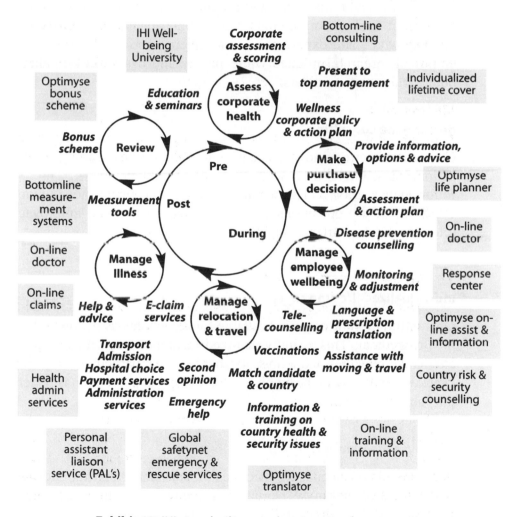

Exhibit 13 IHI story built around customer values

be predicted and obviated, individuals and corporations have the opportunity to perform better and thus feel good, as well as lower their healthcare costs by as much as 50 per cent.[37]

The main set of offerings built around the value adds in the customer activity cycle in Exhibit 13 are briefly explained below.

IHI Wellbeing University

The Wellbeing University was formed to influence and educate independent buyers and executives who were still in the old paradigm of only buying health insurance and looking for the best deal. A global network of leading corporations was brought together to encourage dialogue and share experiences on wellbeing and productivity, do empirical research, produce white papers and cases, and conduct public and private seminars.

Bottom-line consulting

Consulting is offered to assess corporate health policies and provide action plans, including a score against a peer benchmark. This is followed by a report and presentation to top management showing the effects of new propositions on productivity, motivation, employee retention and cost savings, together with the ultimate positive impacts on the value of human capital.

Individualized lifetime cover

Guaranteed lifetime cover is available for the whole family, including post retirement. This is individualized insurance that encompasses alternative remedies and a host of other benefits, particularly regular checkups, in line with the emphasis and ethos that prevention is better than cure.

Optimyse life planner

When people are managing their health, a planning and monitoring tool branded as 'optimyse' begins with a voluntary health assessment, as well as a diagnosis of predisposition to risk, followed by advice and tests when needed, culminating in a personalized health plan with specific targets in line with each individual's personal goals.

On-line doctor

There is access to on-line or teleconsulting, as well as second opinions. Records are kept confidential, separated from the insurance files and business.

Optimyse on-line assist and information

Advice and feedback are provided 24 hours a day on-line, with interventions suggested when appropriate and necessary. In the event of a problem, people are matched and delivered to the correct hospitals and doctors, wherever in the world they and the providers happen to be.

Country risk & security consulting

To reduce the expensive failure rates of overseas assignments, also included is matching people to countries; as well as educating and supporting individuals on health and personal safety issues (from jet lag to allergies, floods to terrorism).

Optimyse translator

This incorporates personalized patient records; kits for travelling for relocation and home use, including prescription and precautionary drugs; translations per country; alternatives and where to find them.

Global safetynet emergency and rescue services

These services range from accidents and loss of baggage to sudden illness or death in a foreign land. The service also covers personal security and rescue services, including assistance with all crises and catastrophes from emergency admission through counselling, advice and information on what to do, where to go and whom to contact, and emergency evacuation.

Personal assistant liaison service (PALs)

On site or remotely, help, advice, liaison and support are given by a personal assistant when people are in trouble.

Health administrative services

Employees are navigated through the labyrinth of administrative, procedural and medical issues related to finding the correct hospital, surgeon or doctor, and dealing with hospital admission procedures, payment and reimbursement.

Bottom-line measurement systems

Reduced absenteeism and stress levels, higher productivity, lower health costs and overall increases in productivity, punctuality, morale and quality of performance are just some of the areas that can be measured with customized tools and techniques to show the impact of the investment on bottom-line returns.

Optimyse bonus scheme

Finally, improvements are rewarded in various ways. Here customers get to accumulate bonus points variously: either they can receive rebates, or these will be allocated to special events like a new baby or retirement, where they can benefit from reduced premiums or added services and cover.

Moving to Implications that Require Action

If the story is grounded in value from the customer activity cycle, a new portfolio of offerings will emerge. In addition, it will provide a very visually stimulating template for examining implications that require action.

This starts with:

- the **skills** that will be needed at the various critical contact points on the customer activity cycle, putting the customer at the forefront of human resource planning and development.

These skills can be compared with the competencies available in house and then an assessment can be made of what new skills base will be needed specifically to deliver the outcome. This would include capability extensions in both specialized new areas and general individual competencies, such as consultative problem solving, communication skills, collaborative negotiation and relationship management.

From that analysis will also come a description of what skills will have to be bought or brought in if they can't be developed in house.

Similarly it will reveal:

- the value gaps *pre*, *during* and *post* that require a network of outside **partners**.

It will also give the oft-claimed but seldom-achieved notion of being boundaryless a chance to come to fruition, because the template makes the connections that lead to the joined-up outcome for customers easy to see and understand. It therefore demonstrates:

- which **silos** have to work in conjunction in order to contribute to customer value.

Then, as the story unfolds still further, it will also reveal:

- the **information technology (IT) network** required to deliver and support actions and interactions on the customer activity cycle, *pre*, *during* and *post*, rather than having to force fit technology to a customer approach after the event.

That often happens when IT initiatives are carried out in isolation from, or unmindful of, the ultimate objective of customer 'lock-on'.

It also provides an easy way to show:

- how the various **initiatives** fold into each other. And how projects need to be linked to deliver the joined-up value on the customer activity cycle.

It will also reveal:

- who the likely **competitors** will be *pre*, *during* and *post*.

Traditional competitor analysis usually comes up with what others making and selling the same products or services are doing, rather than looking for potentially new rivals.

However, it is only when the market space unbundles industry fences and defences, and the new opportunities go onto a customer activity cycle in the chosen market space, that the real rivals can be truly identified.

Finally, a story should quite naturally reveal the **milestones, a list of actions** – time and event pacing, what needs to be done, when, by whom – in a series of interconnected **projects**.

Then it leads to the **new performance drivers and measurements** that will have to be stipulated, and this quickly directs energy and conversations to the numbers.

Size the Prize

Changing the Arithmetic

When a good story is compiled that makes the case for viewing customers as the fundamental source of enterprise value, and presents a picture about what this will take and how it will unfold, be told and sold, it bolsters confidence and enthusiasm. Another breakthrough will thus have been made, driving the process outward and onward.

There is also another part to a compelling case: when the numbers begin to look good, showing how the investment will pay off and how it will lead to greater prosperity that will be long lasting.

Out of the Box and onto the Top Line

First, the arithmetic and some key assumptions have to be changed. Or at the very least, executives need to be made aware of the less than perfect decisions that they could make unless they factor in the flaws of old conventions and outdated views.

Here are the more important ones:

Old view 1
With product focus, it is assumed that money is made by selling unconnected items to as many customers as possible.

Whereas:

New view 1
From customer focus, money is made by selling as many inter-connected items as possible to existing and new customers.

Part of the unconnected regime is vertical integration. This considers how much of what products go through as they are transformed that the enterprise can get involved with. The unified customer approach is to become involved in as much of what customers go through or should/could go through to produce a desired outcome. The enterprise asks itself: how do we become more involved with the activities that customers go through in their activity cycles?

We have already seen several examples of this as enterprises try to create and ride new growth waves. But notice how even packaged goods companies, which have lived and died trying to grind out growth by incrementally adding more brands to their product lines, are seeking to change direction and look for more value components to sell to customers, rather than simply adding more products or brands to their portfolio.

Unilever is a good example and its experience offers valuable lessons. In order to liberate women, customers who are cash rich but time poor and are less willing than ever (even those who don't work) to act like 1950s-type housewives, Unilever launched 'myhome' in 2000 in the UK, offering services to fill the 'household home and fabric cleaning' market space.

This was more than merely a platform for selling more Unilever brands, the number of which had been considerably cut anyway. Instead, the plan was to send teams to people's homes to gather not only dust balls, smudges and other unmentionables in the home, but also the kind of information about people and how they want their homes cleaned that even the best traditional market research could never have revealed. As myhome became more active and present in customers' home routines, and as more and more information about customers' habits and preferences was gathered, the service could become even more involved in those routines.

Some 18 months and 2000 customers later, Unilever decided that the new venture was not profitable enough and so sold it to the Chores Group (now heading for a £20 million goal by 2005) for an undisclosed amount; it nonetheless retained a stake in the venture.[38]

The move from adding more and more brands, many of which were just not making money, to this amazingly innovative new idea is an example of how to grow from becoming more involved in customer activities. Though it was unfortunately terminated, the special lesson to be learned from this example is in the post mortem that came from executives, with remarks like 'It didn't succeed but I still think the trend is there' and 'It wasn't given long enough.'[39]

Old view 2
With product focus, each product had to make a profit in its own right.

Whereas:

New view 2
With customer focus, the justification for making an investment is customer lock-on, because that's what brings the economic benefits that generate the growth and financial success.

Accounting is very adept when it comes to figuring out the cost of products or services. What it is less good at is quantifying the cost of losing a customer, or the opportunity cost of getting only one small part of customer spend because of what the enterprise doesn't do.

To see how much damage this view can cause, one only has to be reminded of M&S's decision not to accept credit cards because an accounting piece of data told top management that it would cost the company around 5 per cent of its revenues. In fact not accepting cards cost M&S much more, because the gaping hole left in the customer activity cycle meant that customers bought less per visit and, for that and other reasons, migrated to other stores where they could use their credit cards.

It wasn't until 2001, during its recovery period, that Marks & Spencer 'lifted its ban on credit cards'.

There were no exceptions at M&S in the old days. If a product wasn't making a profit, the store manager would simply remove it from the shelves (and the spreadsheet columns). Now, as a matter of principle, a range of profits and margins is accepted if a product or service is integral to the cohesiveness of the customer offering.

Or witness what HSC is doing in Germany. In the past, no product got through or stayed in the system at Baxter Healthcare unless a strict rate of return was achieved. Now, like at M&S, a balance between returns is good enough. The justification is whether a product or service produces the value that leads to the lock-on that makes customers lucrative and keeps competitors out.

Old view 3
Monies spent on customers, especially on intangibles, were expensed, expected to show a return quickly.

Whereas:

New view 3
Monies spent to 'lock on' customers, especially if on intangibles, could well be investments in future revenue streams and should be treated as such.

There is a great deal of controversy around what should be regarded as an expense and what should be regarded as an investment. For the moment, the only clarity in the debate is that current accounting systems are out of date and hinder rather than help.[40]

To complicate matters, all sorts of legal implications surround what is and what is not allowed to be capitalized as an investment, because this can significantly change the financial picture.[41] That is exactly the point. Bad arithmetic and old product views and conventions can make it very difficult to create a compelling case, and this can lead to inefficient investment allocations and bad decisions about what to do, what to keep and what to drop.

Increasingly, though, as enterprises enter a world where the engine for growth is the customer and the main ingredients for getting and holding that customer are intangible, more effort is going into genuinely (and honestly) finding a way to align customer focus efforts to more meaningful metrics.

If expenses are made with the express intention of getting customer lock-on and leveraging this later, these expenses become assets. What else can make sense? The opposite point of view, regarding them as costs to be expensed and recovered that year, effectively says that there are no future benefits to be had from, say, brand credibility, knowledge management, skills extension and development, customer acquisition, customer R&D or entrenching customer relationships, whereas there are from other assets, like computers, trucks or chairs.

Baruch Lev, one of the leading proponents of a new accounting metrics that takes into consideration the role of intangibles in creating value, makes the distinction clear. He says, '[only] if there are no future benefits, it is not an asset: it's an expense.'[42]

On a practical level, as the enterprise tries to find its way towards a customer approach, if nothing else being able to make and appreciate the distinction between the old and the new allows executives and investors at least to start thinking and talking on a more profound level. They can thus steer conversations to the important issues, such as:

- What investments are needed to make customers into future growth prospects?
- How can we make the necessary funding easier to obtain? (R&D budgets for products are routine; customer R&D budgets are rare.)
- How can initiatives be given more time so that short-term goals don't wreck long-term potential?

Most significant for the customer-transforming company is that if the arithmetic is changed, however that is expressed, it allows people the freedom and confidence to behave with more innovation-generating gusto. Some of the best-performing new enterprises have done this, reflected in the fact that their market capitalization far outweighs their book value and they have left their predecessors lagging behind.

Unlocking New Customer Currency

Once horizons are opened and the opportunities for adding customer value uncovered through the customer activity cycle, the potential for revenue quickly becomes evident (is there ever a better motivator?).

Unfortunately enterprises still often wrongly believe that getting more involved with customers and offering them more value will cost the enterprise (and therefore customers) extra. They also think that customers, especially those who are more cost conscious, won't be able or willing to pay, so the prize will be diminished.

However, the logical consequence of providing more value and customer lock-on is not that costs go up for the enterprise and so for the customer too. The reverse in fact holds: costs fall, and some of the savings can even be passed on to customers to make the total cost of the outcome more competitive. The top line also increases at the same time, so rather than diminishing, the prize potentially increases for the enterprise.

All of this needs to be built into an algorithm[43] if a compelling case on the numbers is to be made. This is it (see Table 6.1):

> *On the one hand, revenues go up because, once customers are locked on, there is infinite possibility for increasing revenues thanks to longevity, depth, breadth and diversity of customer spend.*
>
> *On the other hand, as customers lock on, operating costs go down because of the new economies of skill, sweep, stretch and spread.*

Let's look at this in more detail.

Table 6.1 The new algorithm

Revenues go up due to:	Costs go down due to:
longevity of spend	economies of skill
depth of spend	economies of sweep
breadth of spend	economies of stretch
diversity of spend	economies of spread

How Revenues Go Up

Longevity of spend

The object with customer lock-on is to make relationships longer and stronger. As the duration of the relationship between the enterprise and the customer grows, more steady revenue streams come from a customer, be it an individual, household or a corporation, farther into the future.

Though realistically the grand ambition is to be able to get lifelong spend, sometimes making an estimate on five or ten years is enough to show the magnitude of the gains that can be expected in assessing potential from this new customer currency.

Patricia Seybold, who specializes in e-marketing, made a guess at what Amazon's customer base could be worth in ten years based on a whole lot of assumptions if history held, which it looks like it will. Her conclusion: by 2010, the amount would be around $50 billion![44]

In addition, with longevity, costs are saved because new customers don't have to be acquired to replace those who are lost, which is what happens when the financial formula centres only on market share. And expenses in managing those customers go down, because set-up and ongoing costs associated with having to get to know them are eliminated or diminish.

BP, for instance, calculated that a one-year, $1.5 million fuel deal for a particular customer had a net present value of between $36,000 and $126,000, depending on the start-up costs. A ten-year deal could boost that same customer currency up to $8.6 million.

Depth of spend

When customers lock on, increased spend doesn't just come from longer revenue streams. As well as buying what they always bought for longer periods of time, customers who lock on also tend to buy more from that supplier. In other words, they give the enterprise more share of wallet; more sites to fill with fuel; more employees to cover with health policies; more Christmas shopping done in that store.

In the past, buyers (especially from the corporate and public sectors) sought out more than one supplier, each providing discrete items, ostensibly to play them off against each other on price or spread their risk lest one failed to deliver. Now, the tendency is to have fewer suppliers, or even one trusted supplier who can produce an outcome that saves the customer the time, energy and costs associated with running around, coordinating suppliers, tendering and so forth.

Breadth of spend

Customer activity cycles are filled with opportunities through breadth of spend. This comes first from the extra value components that are needed to obtain the outcome for specific customers. For instance, M&S went from selling the perfect Christmas turkey to any old customer, to providing the perfect Christmas dinner to individual families that it knows and whose needs it has built into its memory bank.

This breadth of spend is probably what excites executives more than anything else, because here is the potential to build new sources of money for the enterprise that have never before been enjoyed.

For example, the publication of decisions made by US officials on patent applications – the activity on which Lexis Nexis Corporate and Federal Market Division traditionally focused – was only worth 12 per cent of the wider market space Lexis Nexis identified. This concerned the hundreds of millions of dollars that could be realized annually by bringing about a new way of decision making, where answers to patent officers' questions about the novelty of a patent application came from up-to-the-minute databases and systems rather than from slower manual or electronic imaging sources. These databases and systems could be built and fed into customers' routines, updated and maintained.

The extra revenue from breadth of spend may come from existing or new skills developed, bought or brought in. BP uses its finance skills to help customers hedge their pricing, among other benefits. IHI uses its expert doctors to help individuals build, monitor and update their health plans in order to achieve wellbeing.

Alternatively, extra revenues may come from partners in the form of commissions or fees received. Direct Line has become nicely entrenched in breakdown and emergency services, but it doesn't do this itself: it uses a partnering network of franchised dealers that it brings together, coordinates and carefully monitors, and from which it receives a percentage of the business done.

Revenues may also come from separate companies set up to offer the customer a fuller outcome. What Stelios Haji-Ioannou did with easyJet was not only to discount the price of air tickets, but to create a new market by opening up the world to backpackers and cost-conscious people 'who spend their own money' and had not easily been able to afford travel to faraway places before. This initial venture was followed – too aggressively, some argue – by efforts to absorb more of customers' breadth of spend by forming new companies like internet cafés to give them access to the internet while travelling, and easyCar and easyBus so that they could get to and from their destinations.

Diversity of spend

In the old days, in order to grow companies diversified – often to their peril, because they found themselves in unknown territory, which was difficult to manage without any particular theme or unified underpinning to ground them, their resources or their story.

This is quite different from the diversity of customer spend, where when the brand becomes well enough known and trusted by the customer base that it stretches customer spend into new market spaces and so produces adjacent growth. Unencumbered by product thinking and the weight of the mental baggage accompanying it, this has been the stamp of many newcomers such as icons Amazon and Expedia, and other young brands like easyJet or Direct Line.

We mustn't forget Virgin. How many enterprises would have a quarter of its consumers strongly agreeing that it would be the best candidate to run the state pension scheme, compared with only 13 per cent who strongly supported the government in this role? Not many. Yet this brand, said by research to be imbued with the greatest capacity to 'bounce into new sectors', has just that.[45]

Brands are usually stretched as a second-round opportunity after the enterprise has established itself in its market space and achieved customer lock-on. When it does, there are a multitude of adjacent opportunities to capture revenues in new market spaces. For instance, once Chores, to which Unilever sold myhome, got into homes and learned customers' needs and preferences, it could offer them various services to liberate them domestically, including gardening, car cleaning, dog walking, meal delivery and security. It could focus on whatever is a chore for people who want value for time, not just value for money, as well as a better work/life balance.

How Costs Go Down

A customer-focused organization benefits from new economies of skill, sweep, spread and stretch. This, combined with increasing revenues, is what produces the potential for exponential returns.

Here's how it works.

Economies of skill

Much of the value that goes into creating outcomes consists of information, knowledge and expertise. These have characteristics that change the economics involved.

The main point is that they are abundant, so instead of becoming depleted they grow and become more valuable as they are shared, used and reused. Once the initial investment is made in getting to know customers and building the know-how base needed to deliver the values they demand, the cost of updating that information is low. And the cost of serving that customer with better and better outcomes is also marginal, and can even approximate to zero.

In addition, once someone somewhere in the organization knows something that adds value, it can be centrally stored and shared so that anyone in contact with the customer has the benefit of the collective know-how.

It is in this way that IBM stretches its intelligence across the world, as each and every consultant takes the knowledge of all 3000 research scientists with him or her whenever he or she encounters and works with customers, accessing this intelligence with one click on a laptop.

Economies of sweep

While most costs are on the way up, the cost of technology is constantly falling. This is a huge incentive for using technology, provided that it enhances rather than destroys the quality of the customer contact and experience.

If the technology is only used to pull down the cost to the enterprise, it serves no one in the long term. If it enables more personalized outcomes, touching customers and adding value at critical points in their activity cycles at costs that make the enterprise more competitive, it becomes a key factor in obtaining customer lock-on.

Economies also come about because, since the technology has such a wide reach, the enterprise can sweep up large numbers of customers simultaneously at minute additional marginal costs. Plus, customers can go on site and spend as much time as necessary to make a good decision or find the correct information; again, the added cost is small enough to be irrelevant. What is more, having customers who stay connected longer can save the enterprise expense later on, because better decisions are taken up front.

Economies of spread

With investments in customer lock-on increasingly containing resources that are abundant rather than scarce and can thus be used over and over again, the costs can be spread over longer periods of time, rather than only on the immediate transactions. This can make pricing much more competitive and market take-up more rapid.

Also, these investments can be spread over more customers and geographies at very low or marginal set-up costs.

The first corporate assessment done by IHI took a good deal of time, money and resources. Nevertheless, once that methodology had been perfected and the before and after data gathered against which to benchmark the customers' 'corporate health', new individuals coming on stream could be served at a much lower cost.

In another example, moving into value-add services in the UK was strange and difficult at first for the hardcore, product-oriented Unilever. But now, departing from the classic mass-production consumer goods approach, it is taking its expertise and experience and reusing its know-how in Europe and India, where more women are joining the work-force with less time to shop but more money to spend.[46]

Economies of stretch

There was a time when a brand that was strong in one area did not dare to move into another for fear of confusing customers and diluting the image. Some of the more traditional companies still prefer to use new names for new ventures rather than take the risk that their key brand may become contaminated.

However, as we see today, once they have been accepted and respected, brands can be stretched to grow the business. This can be done relatively quickly and cheaply with low or no marginal costs, compared with, say, building more sites, stores or factories, or acquiring other companies for the sake of bolstering market share.

In theory, there are limits to this stretch. Nevertheless, the likes of Amazon, Virgin and others are beginning to show that brands can be much more elastic than anyone could ever have dreamed possible just a decade ago. As the brand gets better known and trusted, the creations that spring from this can cross industries and geographies to absorb more diversity of customer spend, so that expansion can take place at giant savings in the costs of acquiring and serving customers.

Take Virgin. It may have started life as a music retailer, but it has become a brand that can be transferred to common customers across seemingly unrelated categories, from airlines to active health and leisure, bikes to brides, mobile phones to money, trains to travel agencies … the list goes on. Economies of stretch make the acquisition costs and the costs to set up the relationships low or zero, and then the costs to serve the customer minimal.

The Total Value Equation

The value of customer focus can only realistically be sized if enterprises consider customers, and all that goes into making them long-term prospects, as assets that will bring rewards to the enterprise well into the future.

The uninitiated are still perfectly willing to project returns from products and services years ahead because they consider these to be predictable and reliable, even though the time lag between launch and being copied is getting ominously shorter, as are first-mover advantages. (Witness for instance Eli Lilly's loss of the Prozac patent three years earlier than anticipated to 80 per cent cheaper generics as well as stiff competition from Pfizer's Zoloft and GSK's Paxil, or Apple's short-lived edge with its I-pod.)

However, in reality enterprises are still reluctant to project into the future when it comes to customers.

The most common argument against lifetime value, they say, is that customers are simply too volatile: they're always on the look-out for the cheapest or best deal; they have no real loyalty; and they are just plain risky – some more so than others.

Of course, if we're only talking about products and services, 'branded commodities', that can be easily compared and bought elsewhere, then customers will look for the best buy; they will shop around and be looking at alternatives; and they do have more and more access to information, which makes flitting around even easier to do than it was in the past.

With the customer approach, on the other hand, the cost to customers of switching shoots up – not because the enterprise has made it difficult for them to leave, but because it has made it easy for them to stay. It has become indispensable to them, setting up the reinforcing 'lock-on' loop with all the benefits that go both ways.

So built into making that next breakthrough, which is a statement of the contemplated prize from customer focus, is the notion of lifetime value. However, it isn't linear in that the executives simply project a figure for repeat business, with customers buying what they have always bought before, or more, for longer periods.

The object is to connect so closely with customers that as they move, get older, develop or whatever, the enterprise moves with them, or may even instigate the change or progression. The deeper and stronger the bond gets, the more information, knowledge, time and ideas that are shared, the greater becomes the trust. It is then that the magnitude of the value that the enterprise can produce for that individual customer rises and, in return, the customer becomes an increasingly valuable asset to the enterprise.

Doing the Sums

In trying to assess what customers could be worth in the future, certain assumptions must obviously be made because there will always be some fall-off rate. So once estimates of customer worth become specific, they can always be tempered by a risk or loss or hedging factor, or some other weighting measure, probability or set of scenarios.[47]

Nevertheless, in assigning risk and making assumptions, executives should bear in mind that once customers get out of the product buying mode, they start to behave differently and some hidden advantages need to be factored in.

For instance, the stronger the relationship, the more likely it is that customers will have a vested interest in the enterprise, what it does and how well it does it. At the very least, once they are locked on they don't simply leave, even if an error is made: they complain, have a greater tolerance for mistakes, and even help foster the recovery.

They share confidential information and problems, open up their books, offer new ideas and are willing to take on new innovations more quickly. And the enterprise gets higher-ground contact and opportunities for conversations to influence at that crucial, early stage in decision making. Customers don't simply accept the lowest price, they look for trusted suppliers that can provide an outcome. It's no longer unusual to hear comments such as: 'First we choose the supplier, then we worry about the price.'

Also to be added to what customers are worth over time is what the enterprise can learn from them and pass into its knowledge base or on to other customers at very low added cost. It may be even more proactive and offer ideas for improvement. And corporate customers are increasingly helping to suggest and make these improvements work.

When they do, some of the more sophisticated may ask to gain a share of the rewards once these are spread out to other customers, so close does the association become.

Furthermore, when customers in effect do the work themselves and even fill a vital gap in the activity cycle, the enterprise gains materially. Amazon does this with readers who write book reviews for the site; Lego has adult customers as part of its R&D network; and Cisco is well known for saying to new customers: 'If you want to know about our software, ask our customers – they know more than we do.'

Back From the Future

The total customer value approach calculates the net present value of future customer worth because customers are expected to have a meaningful life expectancy, given what the enterprise is able to do for them better than anyone else. How much share of this lifelong value an enterprise can extract is regarded as the true sign and only real measure of customer competitiveness. That becomes the aspiration and target.

Lifetime net present value calculations can be very sophisticated and complex, and the literature abounds in different versions.[48]

Box 6.1 provides a useful guideline for calculating total customer

---

Box 6.1 Total customer value equation

Revenues over a meaningful period from longevity, depth, breadth and diversity of spend – calculated with a built-in risk factor for customer loss
minus
costs of initial acquisition – when there is such a cost
minus
cost of customer maintenance – taking into account the new economies that diminish costs over time
plus
extra gains – like work done by customers, drawing on their knowledge, less time taken to accept new innovations, less price sensitivity, referrals, warnings instead of rebuffs, new ideas for improvements etc.
and as an add-on benefit
less volatility thanks to steady cash flows and working capital, with the potential to reduce the overall cost of capital due to the ability to, for example, self-finance.

value, in which the customer is regarded as an asset from whom benefits will accrue over time.

The most important part of making the case financially as far into the future as executives dare and the institution will permit is that it will influence investment decisions. For some, making the financial case rigorously granular with statistics down to the last decimal point will be necessary to justify these investments.

Others will accept looser approximations, knowing, as Steve Jurvetson, the venture capitalist who funded Hotmail, put it, 'the forecast is a delusional view of reality'. Instead, they will spend time thinking about 'how big the opportunity could be'[49] – and what they have to do to capture it and make it last.

The Engagement

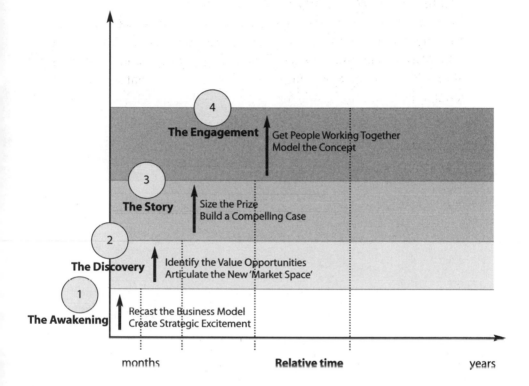

Model the Concept

Getting Buy-In

This is the phase at which engagement needs to take place, with more people from inside the enterprise drawn in. Not only to be enthused and motivated by the new core purpose and the rewards down the road, but demonstrably involved, because what they do fits or will soon fit into the design, delivery or support of the new ways of doing things for customers.

Up until now the 'points of light' and their chosen representatives will have been leading the efforts in order to tap into the positive energies within the organization. Either they will have been deliberately placed in lead positions or they will have gravitated to them of their own accord. But now commitment is needed from a broader spectrum of the population in order to create the momentum that keeps a changing organization moving ahead.

Needless to say, getting buy-in is a never-ending part of any transformation, and making an enterprise customer focused is no exception. What is patently clear from those who have undergone this sort of transformation is that 'selling your ideas, manoeuvring and persuading people is a critical success factor in getting the buy-in'.[50] This is because 'the only thing that really works today and sticks is influencing rather than commanding', with balanced communication that emphasizes both the rational and emotional in equal measure.[51]

What We Know about Buy-In

Ever since the work of Rogers,[52] we know that people take on innovation at different rates at different times. If the enterprise is to stay the course on the way to shifting from a product to a customer approach and move systematically through the step-for-step process that will get it there, the right people must therefore be taken through the phases at the right time.

Enterprises still talk about driving a transformation vertically down the organization, whereas in fact it moves horizontally through one population to another, depending on the risk profile and people's willingness to accept new ideas, irrespective of where these individuals are layered in the organization.

What we also know is that there will always be resistance to change and a portfolio of reactions. People will ask: 'Why do we need to do this at all?' 'Why now?' 'Why this way?'

Furthermore, we know that for the most part these people have an uncanny capacity to resist change, especially (but not exclusively) if they are in traditional settings or large private or public environments. What may be blindingly obvious, even exciting to some people, may bring out negative feelings and behaviours in other people, such as fear of the unknown, failure or loss, disbelief or cynicism, lack of loyalty, even sabotage, or token gestures without real commitment. All of these are to be expected, but need to be managed and minimized.

Categorizing People

Thus we know that people tend to fall into different categories depending on their profile. Part of avoiding the resistance, whether done formally or informally, is inviting and involving people into the process to coincide with the category into which they fit. This is the only way in which frictions and factions can realistically be prevented from blocking the way to progress (see Exhibit 14).

For example:

The small, **activated** category, where 'points of light' are to be found, should exclusively feature during the awakening phase. It is they who will create excitement about the new direction and cultivate the sense of urgency and appetite to break with the past.

The representatives they choose, the allies they seek, the coalitions they build and the team they bring together must consist of enlightened and

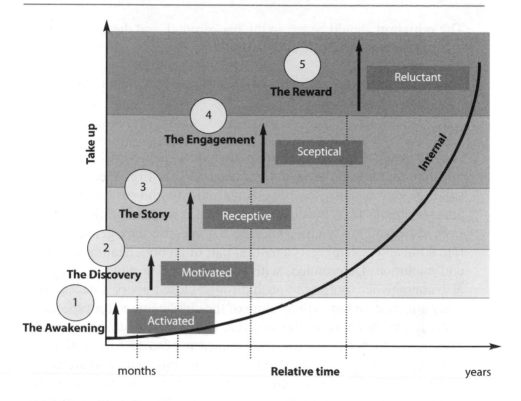

Exhibit 14 Categories of internal take-up through the various implementation phases

motivated people, the next category. They should join the activated and be more prominent during the discovery process, when the market space definition and work on the customer activity cycles are being done.

Once a story is delivered, the bulk of the organization, those who have been **receptive** but were waiting for more clarity and substance, will need to be pulled in and take a more active role. Then they will start to participate in getting engagement from a select group of their close colleagues and customers.

At the engagement phase, when buy-in from colleagues and customers, partners, investors and the media interest begins to swell, it is time to convert and equip the **sceptical**, who until then will still be involved only with business as usual in parallel to new initiatives. It usually won't be until success is declared that they will be completely won over, however – if they remain and survive.

The **reluctant** should be left in the background, and there will probably be a high attrition rate among them.

Here are some of the attributes of each category in more detail.

Activated

A small group is likely to be found, including 'points of light', distinguishing themselves because they react and act first. Generally this
small group not only accepts change quickly and instinctively, but
also sees things from the customer's perspective. They enjoy change,
even upheaval, not for its own sake but because they genuinely see
remaking and reshaping as a natural part of an organization's growth
and evolution. Determined, with foresight and provoking, they are
also courageous: 'willing to push through closed doors if necessary'.
They are creative but, unlike some of the classic innovator types, this
is not to the exclusion of the structure and discipline that they deliberately use to get the concerted balance needed to follow through
step for step. These people also handle ambiguity well and are gifted
at operating in existing milieus while at the same time trying to alter
them. They look for how others, as well as the company, can gain,
which is what makes them ideal candidates for leading customer-
focused transformations.

Motivated

This is a larger and critical group, because its members influence
others, have a high interest level, see the point and want to be integral to the transformation, but only once they have really understood
it. Although typically they will be looking for a defined model and
route, they collaborate and participate as the big picture emerges.
While they look at the details, they don't necessarily demand facts to
support ideas. They admire the activated types and use them as role
models, tolerate change well, and are happy to work for the good of
the whole.

Receptive

These people are more conservative and this can be a large group, particularly in traditional environments. Its members remain preoccupied and interested in daily routines and have to be invited in. They can be engaged, but they will wait for the story to be clearly articulated and monitor the reaction to it. Although they are not as comfortable with change as the activated and motivated, they will cooperate and be prepared to make the leap to commitment once they see evidence of financial viability, moving with caution nonetheless.

Sceptical

Sceptical of customer acceptance, more risk averse by nature, these people will hold out until they see visible signs of success, and will look for evidence and examples of customer acceptance before they commit themselves or release their resources. They will be concerned about consequences for their own patch, and will buy in only when it is clear that the transformation is irrefutably working and they have no option.

Reluctant

These people will only truly buy in once the transformation has gathered sufficient momentum for it to be an irrevocable triumph, though some may never be able to identify with the change. A number may elect to leave early on – and others will simply have to go.

Shocking the Culture

An enterprise may not want to rely only on natural patterns of change to determine when and how people react. To accelerate the pace and shock the culture, it brings in outsiders with a new set of values who visibly demonstrate a different behaviour, hoping in that way to encourage people to change more quickly and 'get their feet out of the cement'.

For instance, no one could have imagined the reaction at M&S when a former retail fashion entrepreneur, the creator of a new and highly successful high street chain and a volatile person known as a maverick who relished saying 'what rubbish Marks & Spencer cloth-ing' was, arrived on the scene, brought in to give advice for exactly that reason.

Marks & Spencer always had rows and rows of the same thing, all at the same eye level. The new retail guru immediately declared that merchandise had to be laid out like a garden, at different levels, with high things and low things that mixed and matched to take the customer through an experience.

'Seeing this, and him in action and head-on, took people way beyond what any normal reorientation or training programme could ever do – it gave them a total break from themselves, which is just what they needed to sign up and get on with it.'

Involving Customers

The engagement stage is also the time when outsiders need to become actively involved. The innovative way of doing things for customers, consisting of the new value-add opportunities, needs to be modelled and made to work. The best way to do this is with customers who themselves become part of the commitment to action and therefore to the implementation process.

The notion of a trial with customers before going to market is not new. But note: this is no pilot test, where the object is to attempt something new and abandon it if the experiment doesn't work. By now a great deal of time, effort and resources will have gone into building a view of the future, knowing full well that traditional methods cannot be expected to reveal this or extract it from customers. Model concepts mean what they say: the enterprise believes in an innovative approach to customers, and then proceeds to get it right and make it work with customers.

In short, it demonstrates the customer concept in action.

Pilot Tests Versus Model Concepts

There are other significant differences between pilot tests and model concepts (summarized in Table 7.1).

Table 7.1 Pilot tests and model concepts

	Pilot tests	Model concepts
Object	Test it and drop it if it fails	Make it work
Commitment	Minimum resources required to start	Put best resources behind it
Choose customers	Who are representative	Who are innovative, prepared to do different, untried things
Timeframe	Defined beginning and end	Can be ongoing – used as laboratory and reference point
Relationship with customer	Keep intentions and experiment low key for fear of failure and exposure	Transparent – jointly make it work
Assumption	Terminate it if it fails	Keep going until you get it right
Intention	Sell to customer when perfect	Do with customer in the spirit of collaboration

The nature of the commitment is also different. In a pilot test generally as few (of the best) resources as possible are used, in order to protect the enterprise in case of failure. Model concepts, in contrast, use the finest people, talent and resources available, because the main object is to do whatever it takes to make it work.

In the classic tradition, a good pilot test would choose a representative market or group of customers with which to work. Average responses from average customers would be the guiding force for a go/no go decision.

In modelling a concept that is customer focused, first there are no average customers or responses and second, even if there were they would not help make any landmark changes. To get the new way of doing things to work, the enterprise will try to engage the most innovative customers, those unafraid of bold moves, prepared to make the unknown happen if they believe in it.

Once again, the enterprise actively looks for 'points of light' with whom to work, this time independent customers, organizations or people within institutions. They are likely to see and feel the need for the new way of doing things, react positively, act swiftly and, like people inside the transforming organization, also be able to influence through 360 degrees, which is particularly relevant in B2B situations.

Pilot tests have a clearly defined beginning and end; indeed, part of the test is to see whether the desired response has happened in a given timespan. Model concepts evolve as people learn and do as they go along, so they can become a kind of laboratory for introducing new ideas. Often working arrangements will evolve, develop and grow far beyond what was originally anticipated or agreed, exposing even more opportunities to work together.

Intentions and experiments are contained and given a low profile in pilot tests for fear that failure may damage the brand. If the pilot doesn't achieve the required response, the assumption is that it will be quickly abandoned. Better customers are preferably excluded from the test to minimize this risk, and only exposed to it once the product or service has been accepted and perfected. Compare this with model concepts, where the enterprise and its customers work together in a transparent way in an atmosphere of sharing and learning in the spirit of achieving results that are mutually rewarding.

Rules for Success

The length of time involved in model concepts can vary greatly, depending on, among other things, the number of markets chosen to work in initially; the number of customers within them; the spread of geographies; the time taken to get customers to agree; and the extent of the commitment. The beauty of doing model concepts with customers is that at their conclusion, and even while they are under way, the new customer approach is in fact being implemented, not merely tested.

So instead of having a thick piece of research to report on at the end, executives can now claim that the new way of doing things is demonstrably working. Also people are given time to adjust to the changes while they are doing something tangible, rather than hearing an announcement about something new and then having to execute it.

For an enterprise like IHI, a group of independent customers or employees could work through how a new health plan can be built up and monitored on the website over a couple of months. In a B2B setting, BP could choose a sector like shipping and work with one or several firms to reduce the amount of energy used by a fleet over a working period of a year; or work with many different sectors simultaneously in order deliberately to capture the overlaps and differences between them.

Getting customers to and through a workshop is the starting point, with the following as the main objectives:

- to test assumptions, interpretations and views on the future direction
- to validate the new concept, captured in the market space definition and customer activity cycle analysis, and fine-tune these if needed.
- to find out what customers consider to be the most important value components or hot spots coming from the string of value adds in the customer activity cycle mosaic.

While validation and feedback are essential, equally pressing is to get customers to buy into the idea of participating in actually modelling the concept, either in its entirety or in part. The overriding objective for the enterprise when entering this vital phase of implementation is to demonstrate proof of the new customer concept and so build showcase early wins. The burden of proof is often greater for people who are trying to make groundbreaking changes than for those who are simply adding additional investment to existing programmes.[53]

So when this does happen, another huge breakthrough will have been achieved. Confidence will be bolstered, which will mobilize the positive energy that accelerates more buy-in inside the enterprise, freeing up more time and resources, which in turn boosts confidence, begetting still more buy-in.

However, a warning: in the same way that success breeds success, so failure will engender expectation of more failure. That can become self-fulfilling and is known to do a great deal of damage to creative initiatives.[54]

That is why it is so essential that some important rules are followed:

Rule 1
Position the workshop as a research event.

The workshops to which selected customers are invited should be thought of and positioned as a research event rather than as a platform to broadcast what the enterprise has already decided to do.

The event should expressly be designed to share opinions and information, allowing active dialogue and rich forums for exchange. The customer activity cycle exercise should be built up jointly, allowing new opportunities for customer value to emerge.

Rule 2
Select customers carefully.

Unfortunately, the biggest (in size or money) customers aren't always the best for a model concept because they won't necessarily be the most forward thinking or collaborative. In fact, they can sometimes be the most conservative.

The questions below should be asked when making the choice of customers in each market:

- Which are the innovators, free and novel thinkers, like-minded and collaborative?
- Which is the most experienced at what it does and will be indicative of, and indeed influence, trends?
- Which is likely to invest time and resources to make it work?
- With which do we have high-level relationships that can be leveraged?

And, especially if customers are corporate:

- Which are likely to provide immediate or follow-on business?

Rule 3
Be flexible on incentives.

Behind this exercise lies the implicit assumption that once your very carefully chosen customers see the gains to be had, they will want to play an active role in making it happen.

Nevertheless, other incentives may be required, because some of the work ahead could involve time and resources that will have to be sacrificed from elsewhere.

These incentives can take many different forms, such as a special price, payment, first-mover advantage or even, in B2B, a joint venture if the opportunity is enticing enough. This is what happened with BP during one of these sessions with a haulier customer, when the idling or rather elimination of idling while drivers slept was exposed as a value add and turned into a new joint venture.

Rule 4
Cover the basics agreement.

Before an agreement to proceed is reached, certain basics have to be agreed, especially who is responsible for doing what, and what resources will be allocated by the respective parties.

It is likely that some unforeseen irresolvable issues will have to be faced along the way, because new ground will be covered and explored, unknown and unfamiliar. This will mean that both parties have to tolerate experimentation in the spirit of jointly finding solutions for longer-term gains.

The gains may even be uncertain. BP could not say exactly what shippers would save if they switched to new ways of managing their integrated energy needs, so it decided to guarantee an upper ceiling and then gainshare in the results.

For all these reasons, if expectations and accountability are agreed at the outset, with transparency as to intent, roles and how to apportion the gains if relevant, the chances are multiplied of solving problems as they arise and of success overall.

Rule 5
Involve the most senior executives.

If high-level executives, including where appropriate the CEO, are not at these workshops at the outset, credibility will be wrecked. If this transformation is indeed to transcend talk on day-to-day grievances or concerns, instead getting into high-ground discussions and being credible on future customer-focused ways of working together, it must have a visible senior executive presence.

When dealing with B2B customers, the same principle applies to the participating institution. If the correct level in the customer organization does not actively support and attend the event, its impact will be lost and the follow-up needed to get the proof of concept may never materialize. As a result, the enterprise may soon be back to discussing products and prices with customers.

Rule 6
Create role models.

Model concepts serve as reference points and role models for other customers. Reputation, trust and credibility expand, which leads to word-of-mouth diffusion and becomes the platform for attracting more customers.

An enterprise may use itself to model the concept: 'You get so much more credibility if you can say we are doing it ourselves.'

Sam Palmisano, CEO of IBM, started by turning his own company into a user of 'on-demand computing' and so become a role model that others could see and follow.[55] So did IHI CEO Per Bay Jorgensen, offering all employees total lifetime wellness programmes starting with the design and monitoring of their personal heath plan, providing intervention in key concern areas from headaches to the customization of canteen food based on the individual's reactions and intolerances to food.

Going for the Hot Spots

While it may sound paradoxical, model concepts are both a new form of customer research and development (R&D) and an opportunity to actually deliver the new ways of doing things or some of the value adds in the customer activity cycle. What is more, these two possibilities are not mutually exclusive, because when the ingredients to produce value are intangible the distinction between development and delivery blurs.

People get engaged during the model concepts to deliver the new and better ways for customers, so they learn, adapt, refine and improve as they go along. If they are working with customers to develop a new value add – say to build a health plan on-line or help to reconfigure a production line in a factory to enable the customer to reuse energy and thus save on costs – a large part of what they are doing is also the actual delivery.

This is foreign to traditional organizations, which research design and develop in laboratories, produce in product or service factories, pilot test in confined areas and then, finally, take the innovation out into the marketplace.

Whether the emphasis and agreement on how to conduct the model concept will be customer R&D or straight delivery is impossible to say, because so much depends on the organization and its circumstances, and no 'one size fits all' formula works. Depending on where the emphasis goes, the ramifications will be different.

Some enterprises may be confident enough to produce benefits for the customer immediately and charge during this modelling period. However, this can be complex if the transforming enterprise has no track record in delivering the values to get the desired outcome and may not even be certain of exactly what costs or gains are involved until it actually does the job.

Other enterprises will be content with viewing model concepts as customer R&D, rather than trying to make them into a paying proposition at the outset. They may decide not to charge at all or reach a special deal, because what they want is to be able to gather expertise and knowledge and then process what they have learnt from customers, using it to build further expertise, knowledge and confidence in areas ranging from high-level consulting to making salespeople comfortable with a new sales approach. They are happy to take the investment into a customer R&D budget and gain in other ways, such as:

- powerfully demonstrating the customer approach in action
- quantifying benefits
- building a body of reusable knowledge
- learning new skills and approaches
- gaining access to information that has never before been available
- showcasing early, visible, promotable wins
- making connections and enhancing relationships.

Finding the Entry Points

Another seeming complexity about model concepts is that, practically speaking, many enterprises can seldom do everything at once, despite the fact that without all the coordinated bits that constitute an outcome they may not be able to deliver the new way of doing things in its entirety.

Don't misunderstand: eventually all of the value gaps must be covered, because leaving gaping holes only means that others will step in and start to gnaw away at customers. Some enterprises prefer to do this right at the outset, because there is no other way to make the promise work.

It is a mistake merely to argue for what is commonly referred to as the 'low-lying fruit'— easy to do and easy to show a quick profit – because this will not challenge executives to do what is needed to genuinely bring about the changes that will lead to lasting progress and success.

In reality, what emerges in personal testimony from executives is that what most enterprises decide to do initially in modelling the concept is a mixture of several overlapping criteria, such as the following.

Demand

A prime rationale for doing the customer activity cycle exercise with prized customers during the modelling is to identify their hot spots. Since these are likely to be the value adds they feel most strongly about for any number of reasons, this is where the transforming enterprise will get the most support and engagement.

Credibility

What do customers have faith that the enterprise can do? This is always raised as a concern. This is not to be confused with a different question – 'What has the enterprise done well in the past?' – as this would get no one any nearer to the new goal. Credibility is more about customers feeling comfortable that the enterprise has either the skills or reputation in a particular area – IHI having a panel of doctors, or BP being well known for in-house risk management and trading capabilities – as this gives credence to the newly enunciated aspirations and working proposals.

Having recognized access to resources and visible commitment from the top achieves the same.

Impact

What intervention(s) will have the greatest impact is another question that executives will typically ask themselves before they decide what to proceed with first. That is why IHI zoned in on preventive services, knowing that without them there can be neither talk nor expectation of a wellness outcome.

Getting in as early as possible in the customer activity cycle is another, equally vital guiding principle in deciding what to do first. How could Lexis Nexis provide relevant questions and answers if databases didn't exist from which to decant the information that customers needed at a moment in time? How could preventive interventions for employees work if a company didn't first have the right policy and approach in place, having benchmarked itself and been scored against other leading companies?

Scalability

What the model projects do is help the enterprise find out how the new way of doing things really works: helping a vessel or production line save on energy, or a retired German person living in Spain stay fit and well, for example. Nevertheless, unless this is transferable to others, what's the point?

Scalability therefore has to be paramount in any decision on where to put the time, money and effort in modelling the new concept. Can it be repeated for sufficient numbers of customers, making the necessary adjustments to suit diverse needs? How can the expertise and knowledge be captured and grown to make it a solid platform from which to gain leverage subsequently? How much can be captured electronically to save on resources and costs to drive market growth?

Measurability

'Can we quantify the gain in order to demonstrate value to customers?' is another critical consideration in deciding where to aim first. The easier it is to measure a value add, the more weight it should be given when deciding where to start.

The ability to measure value should also dictate which customers to include in the model concepts. For example, it would be easy for the Corporate and Federal Division of Lexis Nexis to quantify what a lawyer, salesperson, scientist or acquisition and merger expert could gain by getting information, and to demonstrate this in a model concept. In contrast, to do that for librarians, another market that buys information, would prove much more difficult .

It is the intricate balance of all these criteria that will help executives decide at this important engagement phase which hot spots to hone into. With the object to make the customer connections at the highest level, demonstrate proof of concept and get some early wins that relay the right messages back to the enterprise and marketplace, the stakes will probably never be quite so high in the journey to customer focus.

Get People Working Together

A Passion For Sharing

Getting people to want to work together and turn motivation to commitment and then to action is the next breakthrough to be achieved if customer focus is to take hold in an organization.

The best way of describing the passion for sharing required for this is to say: you know you have it when 'no one wants anyone else to fail or lose because, if they do, everyone suffers'.

That is only feasible if the people working together have a vested interest in giving value to customers and getting that value returned in a mutually beneficial arrangement.

Of course, this will mean being prepared to share the financial prize. That is not something that can be automatically assumed with a product focus, because there the battle for margins on discrete products or services means that someone always has to lose for someone else to gain. This ultimately contaminates relationships and leads to a zero sum gain as the market commoditizes and so sparks the inevitable downward slide.

The Halo Effect

The complete reverse happens with the customer approach. If an enterprise opens up the market by virtue of its ability to see new ways of doing things for customers and makes it happen, it grows and there is a spill-over halo effect for others to grow as well.

When Starbucks made its dramatic debut by finding new ways for people to spend their coffee breaks sitting around in cosy areas, working, reading and sipping cappuccinos, it stole the show from Nestlé, which had been the coffee powerhouse up to then with the lion's share of the market. As a consequence, as Gary Hamel points out, its market capitalization rate was higher than that of the Swiss global giant, although Starbucks had less than 4 per cent of Nestlé's sales revenues in 2001.[56] It continues to grow at 20 per cent or more each year.

However, because of Starbucks' heightened aspiration to create a new customer experience and not simply to do more of the same to steal market share from someone else also doing more of the same, everyone participated in the new success. Coffee was given a new boost in sales not merely in the Starbucks stores, but also in super-markets and elsewhere, innovation proliferated, and the bean enjoyed a brand new image and an extended lease on life. Additionally, margins went up, with 40 per cent of coffee sold priced at a premium, compared to the previous 3 per cent.[57]

Enterprises that understand the long-term implications of the customer approach are happy to share and allow others to benefit. They may have to be patient and wait, but this is in the knowledge that ultimately they will reach a point where their success will be irrefutable and irrevocable if they have the correct partners with which to work.

Take Amazon: although it may not have shown financial returns as quickly as conventionalists would like to have seen, ever since its inception it has consciously sought to allow partners to gain. How else would it have attracted such a network to drive its relentless growth? And gain they have, all 900,000 associate partners. They have links to Amazon on their own site and each time a customer buys something there they get a referral fee.

The enterprise that is trying to push frontiers and invent the future also has to be willing to invent new ways for people in the organization to think about how to work with others, so that sharing can extend beyond money and gains from synergies can be reciprocal.

For instance, Amazon helps associates learn from their interactions with customers. A Performance Tips section shares ideas on how they can sell more items and make even more money from the Web. A Build a Link tool enables associates to easily create a variety of links, tailored to each individual site's content, so they can learn from each other. Amazon also hosts the Associates Discussion Board, where questions or messages can be posted and advice given. In addition, it makes available to partners a Marketing Resource Centre, with expert resources to help them understand better how to market themselves on-line and off.

And the Winner is ... Everyone

With customer focus, the underlying driver is not only to win, but to have the formula and power to make everyone else win as well.

The only way to ensure easy engagement is by building the sense of win–win into the customer concept early on. Baxter's new German venture, HSC, did exactly this, and the move largely accounted for its speedy take-up and splendid success. The considerably longer time that patients could stay at home was designed for everyone's advantage. This was not just to their financial advantage: HSC made sure as a matter of policy that it worked closely with hospitals and doctors in a collaborative spirit, to ensure that the strict conditions of security and privacy protocols were maintained at all times.

Often, what might previously have been conflicting goals between different parties have to be made harmonious to create real win–win. For instance, previously the two nutritional treatments that patients could receive *post* a life-threatening operation were Numico's enteral, given via tubes or drinks, or Baxter's parenteral therapy, received intravenously. These had competed for market share for as long as people could remember. However, as one can imagine, choice of nutrition is all-important to a doctor when a patient is in the advanced stages of a disease and is about to be fed at home. Accordingly, HSC's new homecare initiative provides doctors with options – whatever is best for the patient and the physician. And it sources and delivers the choice, even if it means using competitive products where commissions amount to less.

To become customer focused means that everyone must win and be part of the sum of the whole gain, including customers. In this case:

The patients won because they were cared for with loved ones around them, and saved the hassles of having to go to hospital, stand in queues for medicine, coordinate their various prescriptions and remember when what must be renewed.

The physicians won because they only had to see patients when it was absolutely necessary, and could deploy and distribute their skills more efficiently, retaining control and the freedom to prescribe what's best.

The hospitals won because resource utilization was vastly improved as less bed capacity was used and qualified doctors and nurses had a higher patient/specialist ratio.

The governmental system won because more patients could be passed through the existing capital infrastructure.

The enterprise won because not only has it opened up whole new revenue streams for itself, but its involvement with hospitals has become stronger, as has its involvement with the payment and administrative procedures, thus decreasing costs for all and cementing relationships for the long term.

Mixing and Merging Silos

The good news about the customer focus process is that because it's designed to produce unified customer value, it is all-pervasive. It is not merely another project that can be delegated to one isolated part of the organization with the hope of folding it back in. Instead, it touches on and, indeed, is intended to pull together all of the relevant bits of the organization.

The bad news is that executives always say that *the* most challenging and perplexing part of the process is getting colleagues inside the organization, who for all intents and purposes have been cut off from each other and are preoccupied with their business as usual, to engage seriously in customer focus. This is infinitely more difficult, they insist, than finding outside partners.

Managing the experiences of a diverse customer base (new way) is very different from managing a diverse portfolio of fairly standard products or services (old way). The latter is based on separation for the sake of accounting and accountability. In contrast, whatever goes to make the customer experience has to be connected, based on interaction irrespective of who does what or who reports to whom on the organizational chart.

So coexistence, cooperation and coproduction with internal colleagues or internal partners are imperative, because closed, silo-like structures, mentalities and behaviours cannot produce the unified customer outcomes, and at best may merely result in cross-selling to boost the numbers. Making this breakthrough, when people are not merely motivated but make the unwavering leap to commitment and change their behaviours wherever they may be in the organization, is critical at this phase when customers are being engaged and model concepts are being put into production.

Unfreezing the Silo Mentality

Research corroborates the difficulties of getting people with different kinds of expertise and backgrounds to integrate their perspectives and work successfully together.[58]

Part of the reason this is not so simple is that when people are programmed to make and sell 'boxes', they will be mentally and physically frozen in these product/service silos, thinking about how to count and account for themselves only, without having any superordinate, all-embracing, company-wide customer perspective. This causes still more friction between the factions, as internally efficient as they may seem to be, when they are looked at in isolation.

The following quotes provide illustrations:

Beating up your colleagues was more important than winning in the marketplace (from IBM).

The two main lines, clothing and food, were constantly at war, battling each other instead of working together for common customers (from M&S).

Nor have customers benefited from these artificial slices. Below are two examples.

BP had always worked by strict silo conventions. Each silo would visit some of the same customers and sometimes even compete for them. Though they may not have liked it, customers were bombarded from and had to deal with almost every product division.

Because merchant and card-issuing businesses were separated at American Express, decisions made by the latter arguably worked against the former, causing problems for customers. The fact that cardholders might have wanted to use the card, but increasing numbers of merchants who felt they were being overcharged didn't accept it, could be partly to blame for the downward demand spiral, which knocked the legend off its premium pedestal and has been reflected in its financials, which have lagged behind the averages of its competitors.[59]

Talk often abounds in product organizations about being 'boundaryless', a word and notion accredited to the famous former CEO of GE, Jack Welch. However, it means little until the unified customer view is in place and embraced, because that is something no single silo, discipline, department or division can achieve on its own.

It is only with a common customer concept as a frame of reference, based on the outcome principle, that the various parts of the organization can begin to share information, goals, standards and performance criteria, and so bring the notions of being boundaryless and customer focus to life.

Because it is only then that people can be clear on how they fit together and affect each other and what their respective roles are if the enterprise is to deliver the various value adds *pre*, *during* and *post* in the customer activity cycle.

Any person or unit that doesn't have a part to play in this unified customer outcome – either directly or indirectly – has seriously to question its worth to an organization that is leaping outward to move forward.

Restructuring Around Customers

Getting people to work in conjunction may require a formal restructuring or merging of silos to hold the customer concept together.

Marks & Spencer combined people and units differently to achieve its aim. In the past, silos had been built around the merchandise, from clothing to books, furnishings to financial services. However, how the products or services went onto the physical or virtual shelves was totally unrelated to customers' lifestyle experiences.

Then the silos were merged into teams responsible for joined-up outcomes. For instance, naked stripped beds, bedding, headboards, electric lamps and televisions had all been sold separately before, and the customer bought them in separate transactions and maybe on different floors, or even from different stores. Once the emphasis switched from the bed to the bedroom experience, everything that belonged together became the basis for brand management.

There are many other instances where putting people into new boxes in a formal restructuring is not needed or simply doesn't work, and this is especially true when high-end knowledge-intensive skills are involved. It is greatly preferable to mix and match silos and the people within them in various ways depending on the inner workings of the organization.

However configured or managed, what is most critical is that a mechanism is in place to pull the networks together in order to access the expertise that delivers the values on the customer activity cycle – when and where they are needed.

Ways to Accelerate Engagement

There is longstanding agreement in academic and practitioner circles that in any innovative initiative, the sooner in the process fragmented silos and diverse people work together the better, which invariably accelerates engagement and the pace of change.

It is no different once an enterprise embarks on customer focus. If there is a particular sponsoring business unit that invites others to join in and work with it early on, when the market space is being defined and the customer activity cycles are being worked through, not only can executives' expertise and knowledge be tapped, but it makes them feel more involved and less threatened. Nevertheless, executives warn again and again that this is provided 'you choose the people very carefully – the best people, not just those that can be spared'.

There are other ways to accelerate the kind of buy-in that turns to action.

Demonstrating the gains

This impetus to do things differently together for customers can be strengthened by demonstrating that the silo will not lose and, on the contrary, that it has something specific to gain.

For example, at BP even if a customer's total energy bill shrank due to newly offered consulting advice on how to buy better, use less and reuse energy – something in which supplier and customer gainshared – the silos would still get a deeper share of current customer wallet: a greater number of ships, sites, fleet trucks and buildings to fuel.

There are also other gains from closer and longer relationships, as well as stronger relationships at a higher level. From one executive came this remark: 'Our people were used to dealing with buyers along a traditional selling path. Now they are included in conversations with people at levels and in parts of the organization they would never have dreamed possible.' This changes the nature of the relationships, opening up fresh ideas and opportunities for working together and new business pouring out that could never have been achieved before.

Proliferating the tools

When people actually use common tools and not merely talk about them – whatever these tools may be – they become commonplace, common talk, common practice, making obsolete old preconceived notions, dictates and formulae. This is when the culture begins to switch.

Not only do people start to use the language and the concepts, they also begin to tell the story as if it were their own. 'It's when people start echoing your message, and the story, that you know you have broken through.'

Executives repeatedly confirm that this is the one behaviour that signals that engagement has taken place and that people have accepted not only the direction, but the means to get there as well. Ease and familiarity turn previous reserves and closely guarded agendas into the behaviour platforms needed for the implementation process to begin to take on its own momentum.

Finding the forums to facilitate this is part of the secret.

Lexis Nexis's Bill Pardue says he remembers when he knew he had real take-up: 'All the market owners came to the usual annual strategic investment meeting to put forward their two-four-year resource requests. One by one, they began showing customer activity cycles to motivate their investment requests.... That's when I knew we were there.'

Heralding and celebrating victories

Especially motivating for employees is when victories resulting from the model concepts are heralded and showcased. They are held up as examples, and the positive feedback and public recognition stimulate more people and more innovation.

At Lexis Nexis a successful model concept was executed across businesses to help e-business customers make decisions at Web speed on whether or not to transact with someone visiting their sites. The unambiguous success of this initiative was talked about and deliberately celebrated. As a consequence, it received organization-wide attention.

What soon followed was a myriad of other initiatives, all aimed at the various markets where the risk of customers taking a bad decision was high enough for them to be prepared to seek out and pay for information.

Building a common technological infrastructure

Common technological infrastructures built around a customer experience template form a way of getting people from different parts of the organization to align more quickly.

Lexis Nexis delivered huge amounts of aggregated data to companies and government agencies from hundreds of thousands of sources. In each of the aggregated databases, 'product silos' used to be neatly separated and accountable. Once customers decided to dive into these databases, they found more data and more diversity than anywhere else. But what they wanted was to make an important decision quickly, and they neither knew nor cared where, or from whom, this information came.

Lexis Nexis is now organized around what the customer does, and technology interfaces are designed to get to those people with a common set of activities the exact information they need to take an important, even career-making, decision in real time.

Governments are beginning to move in the same direction. In the United States, for instance, there has been a significant shift to improve collaboration among states through common customer technology infrastructures. From the state of Pennsylvania comes this remark: 'We need to go to city hall to get a permit for remodeling our house and then to the lumberyard for the materials to do the job. We go to one place to get fishing gear and another to get a fishing license.' By linking agencies and private companies involved in customer experiences, the government is getting the relevant parties to start working together to provide a better, integrated service.[60]

Linking performance to customer outcome

Linking performance criteria to achieving a customer outcome is a powerful motivator in changing behaviour. Unfortunately, all too often product-focused enterprises are afraid to relinquish performance metrics that showcase sales of their core items, and so hold on to the old schemes, confusing and confounding people and seriously holding up progress.

Once organizations do let go of what is often the last vestige of product-mindedness, they find the transition to customer focus that much swifter. For example, in the old days business was largely subscription-based at Lexis Nexis; now the fact that performance metrics are linked to the return the customer gets from the use of the information has significantly altered how people think, and what they do and prioritize.

New roles in customer management and in performance contracts may need to span not merely silos but also geography. BP illustrates this: it has switched from single-product or single-region performance contracts to ones where rewards and recognition are global, spanning silos. Highly skilled individuals sit outside of any single business unit structure, accountable to someone who works cross-stream, reporting to the highest level.

Finding External Partners

With a customer-focused view of the world, the driver for engaging external partners is to fill a gap or gaps in the customer activity cycle. It may be as simple as linking to a mapping technology on a website, as easyCar does to help customers get in and out of cities, or more complex, such as when IHI calls on an international expert in security to give a corporate customer advice on how to protect an employee from a dangerous situation in a foreign country.

Essentially, this is irrelevant to the product model of doing business, where partnering is more about improved supply chain management than about the management of customer contact and delivery, which is what an enterprise moving to embrace the customer approach is trying to achieve.

Here partnering will typically occur when the enterprise doesn't itself have adequate or appropriate infrastructure, knowledge or skills. For example, because the new sophisticated approach of migrating people from hospitals after surgery back into the community for care would be complex, the German executives at Baxter knew that they could never make it work on their own without partners. So they formed a joint venture with others, including Numico, an expert in enteral nutrition, and a company which had been doing work in after-care service in wounds, selling patients wheelchairs, beds, bedpans and so on, and already had an infrastructure in place: 17 locations situated all over Germany and 170 nurses calling into hospitals and caring for seriously ill patients after an operation.

The point is that these companies could never do alone what they could achieve together – offer a totally complementary set of skills to supply a comprehensive, joined-up post-operation outcome.

Alternatively, partnering will happen when the enterprise doesn't want to make an investment because someone else can do it better and/or quicker for customers. 'It's what's good for the customer that drives our decision on whether to partner or not. Anything else makes no sense and gets people thinking about themselves again, instead of what's happening out there.'

Because of the potential (mentioned earlier) to locate criminals by finding out who has taken out pilot's or driver's licences in a particular area, when Lexis Nexis ventured into its new market space it partnered with a firm that collects and aggregates licensing databases, instead of trying to build these itself.

Triggering a Positive Growth Spiral

The further afield an enterprise ventures in redefining its market space and consequently its new core purpose, the more likely it is that it will need to partner with external players. In addition, once an enterprise has achieved customer lock-on and begins to get second-round opportunities for diversity of spend in new market spaces as we have discussed, it will often partner rather than try to build the skills that others already have, preferring to harness its own resources to enable it to invest in customer information, interaction and relationship building. Thus it leverages the skills of others to get support for growth for its brand in a positive, upward spiral.

For instance, having got itself firmly into the *pre*, *during* and *post* stages in customers' auto spaces, Direct Line is getting diversity of spend by stretching into their home space, offering insurance to cover property and personal belongings. However, rather than investing heavily in this home insurance, instead it decided to partner with Churchill Insurance, a company that is strong in the area. Although both enterprises are under the ownership of Royal Bank of Scotland, it is Direct Line that gets the customer cachet.

Partnering in this way not only leads to more spend per customer and therefore top-line growth, but it saves the enterprise time and money, both of which can be important in speeding up customer buy-in for a new, innovative way of doing things. This is clearly important in gaining even more partners, making the experience even richer for customers.

Consider what Expedia did. It began to partner with well-known hotels to give customers choice at different price points depending on their specific profile. By drawing more customers in it gave itself a powerful basis for attracting airlines at better prices, a benefit that it then passed back to customers, thus attracting still more customers, as well as more partners.

Savings can also occur when resources are combined. By sharing back-office services or combined information technology with Churchill Insurance, Direct Line could not only improve the quality of the customer experience, but also make its price more competitive, thus further fuelling take-up by customers and attracting more players to join forces, triggering a positive growth spiral that others would find difficult to beat.

Forming Extended Enterprises

The enterprise is no longer a whole mass of different, unrelated product and service factories, or distribution or processing channels, that are legally owned by the same organization. The new extended enterprise is made up of a constellation of partners, as Peter Drucker[61] has expounded, held together by a common core purpose and set of customers.

It's what they do and accomplish in the marketplace *together* that binds them, not to which legal entity they happen to belong.

There are a whole variety of possible formats and formal working arrangements for executives viewing partners as a possible extension to their enterprise. Alliances and joint ventures, franchising, minority stakeholdings or straight outsourcing are the most popular.

Some enterprises prefer more informal collaborative schemas where people work together when the occasion arises. Or they may simply plug into a network of specialists to supplement their skill or knowledge base when needed.

Partners collaborate to build a better customer experience. Research on practice confirms that, irrespective of the arrangement, the stronger this collaboration, the more each party will gain.[62] This is for some very simple reasons, including the fact that it is more flexible so it doesn't hamper innovation.

In reality the collaboration could range from a minimal exchange of essential information when necessary, through the limited ability to access each other's customer data information and databases, to the much more ambitious open sharing of this knowledge and integrated databases, processes and relevant resources. That may require more effort and time initially, but it pays off in the long run.

A Matching of Equals

External partners are fundamental to the delivery process and therefore to getting the new concept accepted and into the hearts and hands of a larger customer population. Getting the right partners may go beyond merely filling in gaps: they can also enhance credibility and image in the initial phases of implementing a customer-focused new venture or transformation. All of this adds up to the achievement of yet another breakthrough challenge, further fuelling the process.

What this means to the transforming enterprise is that decisions on which outsiders it should work with are far from trivial. Some enterprises go so far as to talk to customers first. Baxter, for instance, interviewed patients, hospitals and surgeons in order to get their opinions before deciding on partners for its new German venture.

Here are some of the criteria that executives say are vital in making the choice:

- Are they excited and motivated, like-minded in terms of the customer concept and direction?
- Can they work at our pace?
- Do they understand and believe in the concept of lifetime customer value?
- Are they prepared to collaborate for the good of the whole, so generating win–win for all?
- Are they willing to share information and contribute other resources like time, energy and expertise (and even funds when relevant) to make the new way of doing things work?

And, especially if customers are corporate:

- Are they seen as leaders who will influence and attract others?

Foremost in what works and what doesn't if true customer focus is to be implemented is that external partners have to be regarded as equals rather than merely suppliers. This is reflected in close relationships, motivation and collaborative behaviours, not simply transactional behaviour (see Table 8.1).

Some examples follow.

Table 8.1 Partnering relationships: what doesn't work and what does

What doesn't work	What does work
Control and domination	Trust
Owning everything	Having access
Only our brand	Co-branding, implicit or explicit
Providing specifications	Working to common service levels and standards
Placing contracts	Jointly developing and co-innovating

Control and domination versus trust

Previously, enterprises controlled and dominated suppliers from which they bought goods and services as inputs to their businesses. They probably could have bought these anywhere else, especially if they had buying clout and a high-end user profile that added to their power base. The net result of this was invariably contention and controversy, with players often pulling in opposite directions in complete disregard of the impact on end-customers.

Now, not only must enterprises work together for a common purpose with end-customers placed squarely at the forefront of decision making, but they must do so with others whose brands may be as powerful as their own. With this comes the need for trust. This means transparency, which can take many forms but, most importantly, requires a clear understanding of who does and has responsibility for what, and a respect for who owns what, particularly customers, thereby avoiding trespassing.

When Amazon uses a courier or postal service to deliver its books around the world, it outsources the service in purely transactional terms. However, the delivery service can be as important to the outcome as the choice of the book itself, and since this is the only physical contact the customer has in the entire experience, any default could seriously reflect on the Amazon brand. Amazon counters this by insisting that if something does go wrong it is to Amazon that the customer makes recourse, and Amazon is the one that takes on the responsibility of rectifying the situation and therefore retaining customer lock-on.

Owning everything versus having access

By owning everything the enterprise protected itself, or so executives used to think. It also kept information, knowledge and technology infrastructures proprietary for fear of losing control. That is no longer the case. Since customers don't care who possesses what provided they get the end result, having to own everything is no longer a priority. A proprietary system isolated from a collaborative network and unlinked – no matter how proficient – can be distinctly disadvantageous to achieving the integrated concept that is so paramount to implementing customer focus.

Scientists, lawyers or teachers don't want to have to click into libraries and files from 50 different US states to find the answer to a question. Lexis Nexis gives customers access to the best and most relevant information so that they can make a presentation, win a case or develop a breakthrough product, irrespective of where that information originates. 'Which is quite amazing if you think that in the past everything had to be proprietary and owned,' as one executive put it.

Only our brand versus co-branding

When co-branding is used merely to extend reach and save costs, without changing anything at all for the customer, it becomes nothing more than another product-focused, transactional tool. The coming together of airlines and credit cards is a classic example of two industries where the heritage companies, lagging seriously behind in the race for customers, are using this tactic to get people to fly more with those airlines and use the cards to pay for those flights. In this kind of situation, co-branding is not necessarily employed to enhance the customer experience.

With customer focus, co-branding is much more subtle and much more challenging. Two enterprises, sometimes of equal stature, come together so that both can land their value add(s) on the customer activity cycle.

The customer is effectively dealing with two or more enterprises, each of which works under its own brand, though only one has responsibility for managing and coordinating the overall outcome.

Because IHI included personal safety in its definition of wellbeing, it needed a strong partner to work with to help corporations

and their employees minimize danger when travelling to high-risk regions of the globe. Its choice was Control Risk Group, internationally renowned specialists in everything from country risk analysis to corruption, kidnapping and terrorism. The personal safety services that it delivers are part of an effort by IHI to co-brand on and off its website.

Co-branding may even entail working with competitors. For example Amazon has Borders as a partner in the United States so that its customers who either like going into bookstores or want to pick up their books themselves, rather than wait at home for a delivery, can do so. Borders gains by getting potential new traffic and Amazon fills an important value gap.

Provide specifications versus working to common service levels and standards

Providing specifications works fine when dealing in discrete products and predictable and standard customer needs. However, when real-time actions and interactions are required, many of which may be personalized and complex, this simply doesn't work.

With customer focus not only do participating players need to have a unified view of the customer, the customer has to have a unified view of the partners. This can't work unless service levels and standards are common and in place.

Direct Line is a case in point. It uses over 300 garage owners and dealers who go out to help customers in an emergency when their cars break down on the road. The members of this network use the Direct Line brand umbrella, and service levels and standards of practice are set and precise, such as how long it should take to answer a call, how long it should take to get to the roadside scene, how long it should take to repair the vehicle, that customers should be provided with alternative transportation, and that they should be billed automatically on their card to save as much time, cost and hassle as possible.

Placing contracts versus jointly developing and co-innovating

Whereas previously a supplier's compliance was what kept a deal ongoing – 'contracts were placed and they were simply told what to do' – commitment is required when enterprises seriously want to be part of the new customer concept, updating, upgrading and constantly innovating to reap lifetime customer benefits. The alternative is suffering the defeat of a lost sale due to price, or one-off deals that have to be continually renewed.

For example, when the US legislature wanted a way to visually understand the connections between individuals and companies sitting on common boards, owning equity and so forth, in order to find possible criminal links, Lexis Nexis put together its search engine and data with a creative partner. Together they came up with a tool so that these law enforcers could easily and visually depict the common links, rather than having to wade through standard checklists.

The closer the collaboration and exposure that partnering enterprises have to one another, the more likely this joint development and co-innovation effort is to continually enhance customer value, with the risks and rewards both shared.

The Reward

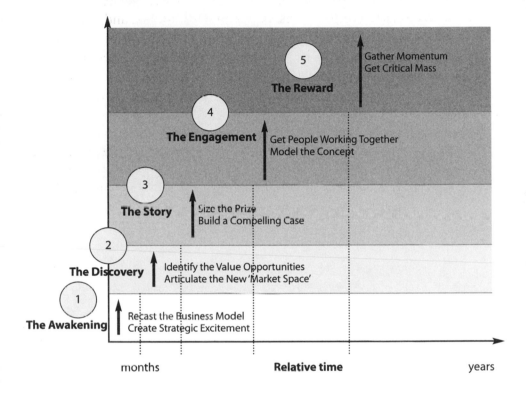

Get Critical Mass

Compounding Customer Take-Up

When an enterprise has reached the stage where there is a critical mass of take-up from customers for the new way of doing things, a breakthrough will have been achieved that finally unlocks the promised exponential rewards.

This starts to culminate in the fifth and final phase. After this critical mass comes a groundswell, as the market buys into the new concept innovation.

Thanks to word of mouth, intensive marketing and carefully crafted methods to entice people in at the correct time, the scale builds. In terms of numbers this scale, fundamental to making the economics work, can be anywhere from 5 to 50 million customers, depending on the enterprise.

Those who are still wedded to a product focus will of course routinely get this kind of scale from making and moving a certain number of products or services year in and year out. Being inwardly facing, they will also be looking to centralize activities in order to achieve the benefits of production and administration scale. Nevertheless, not only does this seldom bring in the returns, it is also known to stifle innovation.[63]

Alternatively, they will be trying to scale up only where and when they think they have sufficient demand, begging the real question: how do we *create* a market?

With customer focus, the enterprise will get scale from quite another source: making investments that enable it to attract and then lock on *more* customers, thereby getting *more* of their spend over *more* time. This comes about because the organization provides its customers with value, and invests the time, effort and resources to make that fact known to them and others.

Making the Brand Contagious

Some of the take-up will already have been accomplished through the model concepts. If they are clever, established enterprises will have intentionally selected a group of customers – the 'points of light' within their market domain – and used them to energize the conversion process. Newcomers bringing customer focus into a stale industry will, by definition, attract the early adopters who spread the word, and influence others through their changed behaviour patterns and affiliation.

After modelling the concepts and their adoption by sufficient early entrants comes the critical mass of take-up, and then the new way of doing things becomes infectious and more customers respond. This is the turning point for the transforming enterprise. Conversion will spread very quickly in the marketplace.

That is how the brand goes from being indispensable to a select number to penetrating the wider market. The customer then receives and returns the kind of value that makes the relationship long-lasting and mutually rewarding.

Although getting critical mass and then scale is fundamental to success, there is no easy way of doing it. This is mainly because, however beneficial the new concept is to customers, with few exceptions it will involve changes in attitude and habits, and this invariably has to be played out over time.

Marketing certainly won't get the compounding effects of take-up and make them last if it is based solely on traditional hard-sell promotion and short-term broadcasting techniques. More is required: the intention has to be first to make a genuine investment in winning over customers to the new way of doing things. Then once the investment has been made, the object is to become ever more involved with individual customers, interacting and giving and getting information to and from them so as to bring about ongoing and ever-improving value.

Whether the brand exists or is new, if it is geared to a new way of doing things, it has to earn the market's credibility and trust to build demand. This means becoming indispensable to customers because the concept works and delivers the outcome: only after this can the brand become infectious to a wider audience.

In other words, the brand's credibility and popularity arise from what customers get, not merely from creative marketing campaigns.

A Brand by Any Other Name?

Some established brands are well placed to make the leap to a model based on unified customer value, but they may be reluctant to use their brand name in case it contaminates their core business.

This happened to Unilever, which decided not to use its own branding on myhome. Nevertheless, having struggled with an unknown name to build scale quickly enough, it reversed the decision and decided to used one of its well-known product brands to stretch into Persil-branded laundry and dry-cleaning outlets in UK supermarkets. It has used another well-known brand, Ponds, for its Ponds Institute in Spain, a chain offering beauty and facial treatments. And it launched a similar service, under the Lakme-Lever brand, to the growing middle class in India.

Some of the best examples of building and scaling brand for new ways of doing things come from newcomers. As a consequence, they may remain outsiders, but they don't stay newcomers for very long.

For instance, despite its eccentricity it is not just hot air that gives Virgin the brand power that has enabled it to attract customers and their money, no matter which way the enterprise turns in pursuit of growth. It, like others, has realized that the brand is in the experience, not simply an offshoot of a whole lot of disparate products and services.

So in the airline business Virgin Atlantic became the new standard bearer for an individual passenger's unified experience *pre*, *during* and *post* on long-haul flights. Its latest commission to the aircraft manufacturers is to build jets that defy most people's notion of air travel: instead of a passenger being assigned one seat for the duration of the journey, the new aircraft, still in its early design stages, will be more of a floating five-star hotel. Branson aims to have a cinema room for those who want to watch films; a work space with computers, phones, faxes and internet connections; a bar area for those want to gather and chat over a few drinks; a restaurant area – or several, in fact, since some people like haute cuisine while others prefer a salad bar; as well as a gym and sleeping areas.[64]

While this will surely attract a raft of customers to the Virgin banner and firmly associate in customers' minds the enterprise as first mover in the new way of flying, if we go back to basic principles of customer focus this is insufficient to get customer lock-on and scale. Others will soon follow, and the battle for market share to take people back and forth across the oceans will simply continue.

For a brand to become contagious and get the compounding effect that gives it lasting scale and an unassailable position, every resource and opportunity must be used to interact with customers so that they get the personalized value that achieves an outcome that is constantly updated as customers, technologies and environments change.

Making it Easy for Customers to Say 'Yes'

Making it easy for customers to say 'yes' accelerates take-up, especially if long-standing habits have to change. One of the reasons the UK government's pharmacy reform initiative – making pharmacists more responsible for patient medicine management to ease the considerable waiting and wastage in the National Health System – has been successful is that neither patients nor pharmacists risk being penalized by adopting the new way of doing things.

Pharmacists, now more involved in their local communities in the UK as part of the government's reform initiative, are responsible for identifying symptoms among certain minority groups in their area – predispositions, say, to asthma or diabetes – in order to help prevent the disease or assist people in complying with prescribed medications and recommended lifestyle changes.

Although both pharmacists and customers have to switch habits, this is countered by several deliberate moves to encourage them to do so, including the following:

- Patients who still need to go to their GPs despite a pharmacist's initial intervention by way of advice or medication are put on the hospital fast track and given rapid access to doctors. This way they aren't penalized by having to go all the way to the back of the queue.
- Pharmacists take on more of the role of consultant and may in the process end up dispensing less medicine – their bread and butter in the past. However, now they earn consulting fees from the government and, irrespective of whether they prescribe or provide medicine, they are paid these fees by their Primary Care Trust (PCT).

- Moreover, Webstar Healthcare, the designer of the interactive systems, is in charge of training and of establishing the new contracting agreements with the PCTs, so eliminating the administrative hassles of being paid and speeding up the acceptance rate.

Making it easy for customers is more about mastering the art of thinking differently than about being operationally adept. It's not merely that Amazon has a technological capability that is driving it forward, making the brand synonymous with popular culture. It's that it consistently makes it easy for people to become involved in its multifaceted machinery: entering the site, navigating, ordering, obtaining the goods, complaining, getting rectification, sending a gift to a friend, chatting, giving an opinion, buying a second-hand book.

Most people would argue, as indeed some of the management at Amazon did at first, that letting customers buy second-hand is bad business because it cannibalizes sales. However, Amazon's data intelligence tells it (because it thinks differently and asks the question) that once customers can easily buy second-hand books and experiment with unfamiliar authors for whose works they wouldn't be willing at first to pay the full price, they go on to buy new books by that author.[65]

To drive its growth Amazon uses the same principle for retailers whose sites it is developing. It makes it easy for them to grow their business on-line by providing them with a technological platform that is simple for their customers to use. Though the retailers maintain their own branding 100 per cent, the layout of the site is deliberately very similar to Amazon's, so that customers, most of whom are familiar with the Amazon site, can easily navigate their way round it. Similarly, Amazon's patented one-click technology is also available to the merchant's customers, so that once their details – credit card preferences, mailing address, invoicing address, friends' addresses and so on – are in the system, they don't have to fill them in again every time they place a new order. The system also recognizes customers and, based on previous purchases, will offer suggestions that might be of particular interest to that specific customer, all to improve the merchants' ability to easily get their end users' purchase rates up. If a problem does arise, Amazon will offer recovery services to the merchant suppliers.

Ways to Speed Up Customer Acceptance

There is no single or simple way to get take-up quickly and make it long-lasting. However, there are several other moves that do contribute significantly to speeding up customer acceptance at this stage so that the enterprise can begin to reap the rewards:

Making it easy on the finances

Making it easy on the finances is not to be confused with offering free goods, loss leaders or discounting – all old product concepts. The aim here is to make people less reluctant to try something new, even if the outcome is not entirely clear at the outset. Here are some examples.

HSC doesn't charge for the initial home assessment it performs when it takes on post-operative patients to help them recover fully at home. Nurses go round to patients' homes and examine them to see if they have the necessary physical facilities and emotional support for post-operative home care; if they don't, whatever is required is obtained for them without charge.

To get on-demand computing off the ground, IBM asks customers to pay only when they turn the computer on. Using computing without buying the machines is part of IBM's story, which dovetails nicely with turning computing power into a utility, available at the lowest possible cost, where people have automatic access to exactly what they need when they need it, but pay only for what they use, in line with an overall need in the marketplace to cut down on unnecessary expenses.

Educating customers

Customer-focused enterprises don't simply meet or exceed customer expectations: they mould them. Customers adopt concepts they have not yet encountered and may never have imagined possible.

So part of getting critical mass and market take-up is riding the paradoxical waves of educating the market while at the same time creating and compounding it. Nevertheless, education requires investment.

Play is an essential part of a child's growth. When play is combined with learning, 'it grows the human spirit and encourages imagination, conceptual thinking and creation'.[66] Lego's venture into retail stores is not an attempt to vertically integrate and control the distribution channel to sell more boxes, another old product idea. It has set up stores around the world, including in the United States, the UK, mainland Europe, Australia, Singapore and Japan, expressly to make these stores part of the brand experience, where customers can come to terms with how to interact with the play materials, software and interactive technology. In these educational settings, say executives, Lego has found a way to communicate and educate its customer population, making sure they understand how the concept works and getting them engaged beyond what they expected they could do. This is an integral part of the Lego ethos, but something that could never happen in a traditional store setting.

There is no way out if the rewards of customer focus are to be realized and endure. If the enterprise fails to educate the market, it may never get the take-up that makes the new way of doing things accepted and standard.

Look at what's happened with Monsanto, which has had enormous trouble getting biogenetic ways of farming understood and accepted in Europe. Despite no real proof that genetic modification is unsafe, there has been massive resistance among governments and farmers, with 70 per cent of the consuming public saying they don't want to eat this kind of food at all.[67]

Quantifying the customer benefits

Closely allied to education is demonstrating value to customers, so drawing them in early and swiftly. Here the enterprise must actually be able to show that customers are better off with it rather than without it. Needless to say, it's only when this happens that the innovation really takes hold, and new ways of doing things begin to become part of customers' daily lives and routines. This is when the implementation moves into a new gear and starts to show returns.

IHI uses its Wellbeing University as a vehicle to educate the corporate market and also to quantify the benefits to be gained from investing in wellness programmes. While corporations mostly still look at pulling down direct health costs, they could instead be getting huge returns on their investment from interventions that not only save them costs (both direct and hidden), but also bring in extra monies from increased productivity and performance. Together with leading global corporate lights and experts, IHI's various education initiatives include joint research, forums and publications.

Quantifying the benefits requires two things:

- Looking at total costs over time; in other words considering not merely the cost of getting the core items, but the cost of getting the outcome. Additionally, the enterprise has to demonstrate how the customer can save – in terms of time, money or hassle – by doing things differently, or how the value of the outcome more than compensates for any additional spending involved in getting it.
- Collating both 'before' and 'after' baseline statistics, as well as statements verbalizing the intangible benefits, 'often many times as important as the monetary'.

Sometimes showing evidence of value can only be done when the concepts are being modelled with key customers. This is because the benefits are difficult to predict before the new way of doing things is tried and tested and its value is demonstrated in action.

Think about trying to quantify exactly what an individual would gain from preventive health interventions before the related database has been developed. It wouldn't be possible. Or saying exactly what a litigating lawyer, scientist, patent officer or insurance or claims assessor could gain from better/quicker decision making. Or what a manufacturer could get by being able to react to the subtlest of changes in the marketplace thanks to consulting and on-demand computing – a challenge in quantification that IBM now faces.

This doesn't make the customer concept or story any less compelling. However, it does mean having to build new capabilities that can produce tangible and intangible evidence of customer value, instead of merely intricate cost calculations on products and services.

It also requires being willing to live with uncertainty, working interactively and collaboratively with customers at this stage to quantify the tangible benefits. For the intangibles, it entails jointly building a list by putting words around some qualitative statements.

There is one proviso: the basis of the equation must be based on the *customer's* perception of success.

This is what Lexis Nexis Corporate and Federal Market Division did. Executives sat down with insurance claims assessors and asked them for their definition of success. As it turned out, this was the amount of times that fraud had been identified and money recovered. Then executives obtained 'before' success rates, looked at the information Lexis Nexis has injected into the customer activity cycle during critical decision points in the customer's workflow, analysed 'after' success rates, compared them with the 'before', then was able to build a formula to quantify its contribution.

Managing the 'Push/Pull' Rhythm

Critical mass is needed both internally and externally.

Insiders influence one another, and together their successes which are highly profiled set an example for others who in turn become more comfortable, confident and courageous.

Getting the 'points of light' and some of the activated group to see the logic and feel strongly, in the sequence that John Kotter calls see–feel–change,[68] and then behave differently is the first milestone in an ongoing process of pulling the correct people in at the correct time to adopt the new way of doing things for customers.

Then come the rest of the activated group. Tuned in and turned on, they buy in, attract the motivated group and then suddenly, enough people – around 20 per cent of the population[69] – start to think and behave differently, drawing still more people in. As a consequence, the speed of take-up gathers, culminating in accelerated internal buy-in, which drives the internal take-up curve at an exponential rate (see Exhibit 15).

Once the model concepts begin to show results, customers begin to buy in to the transformation and affect the opinion and behaviour of other customers who watch, listen, read and are influenced, triggering external take-up.

This external exponential curve mirrors the internal curve (see Exhibit 15), where the same well-known principle of conversion operates as is used in some of the most celebrated cases of best practice innovative change management in the public and private sectors.[70] When the beliefs of a critical core group of people have been changed, their energies begin to infect others, and once that happens others quickly convert.

Expanding Positive Energy Movements

These two expanding movements of energies move in tandem as people inside influence each other, and as customers and other interested parties outside do the same.

The two streams also affect one another, making them

inexorably linked and reinforcing the fact that the systematic timing and management of their interconnecting rhythm is so important in successful implementation.

This fact is often missed by executives, who manage internal and external buy-in separately, as two distinct activities. This can put them out of sync – the enterprise can't get the market to take what it is ready to give, or the market can't get from an enterprise what it is ready to accept.

It also cuts off the positive feedback dynamics between internal and external forces, which could otherwise be used to power the process. This positive feedback comes about because of the synergistic effects of the interplay between the internal and external energy streams. They nourish each other in a rhythm of 'push/pull' that, when carefully managed, can help to move the implementation process on to achieve its critical mass.

Effectively there are three dynamics at work. Let's take a look at them in more detail.

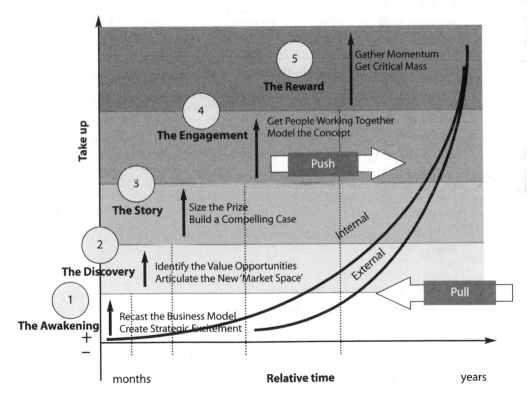

Exhibit 15 The 'push/pull' take-up

Dynamic 1: Inside 'push' rhythm

When the model concepts with customers begin to show proof that the new approach is working, more traction is created among insiders and more people start to use the concepts and language, institutionalizing the customer approach that then becomes manifest in new thinking and behaviour patterns. As evidence of success from early wins grows and is heralded, enthusiasm and confidence levels increase throughout the organization, producing a *push* to do more, more quickly.

Dynamic 2: Outside 'pull' rhythm

Externally, as the model concepts start to take shape and/or early adopters begin to buy, demand compounds to create a *pull* from the outside. Add to this the increased press coverage, heightened interest and involvement from partners and developers, and curiosity and receptiveness from investors, and the demand accelerates so that it finally produces sufficient critical mass of take-up through the marketplace.

Dynamic 3: 'Push/pull' rhythm

The more the support and engagement grow inside, the greater the chances of early victories, because more people and resources are committed and people discover more and more things to do. This internal *push* in turn boosts involvement and interaction with customers, which increases their commitment and the *pull* from the external world, which reinforces the appetite and case internally for more time and investment.

In essence, these positive feedback loops result in a rhythmic flow of energy and support

*through the enterprise
and through the markets*

and

*from the enterprise to the market
and back into the organization.*

Ultimately, the internal and external take-up curves converge to make what was new *the* standard among increasing numbers of insiders and outsiders, building the required critical mass and more.

Gather Momentum

Leveraging the Investment

The ultimate breakthrough occurs when this take-up has happened: the internal and external 'push/pull' rhythm has produced enough unstoppable momentum to generate the anticipated financial rewards, usually starting at around the 18 month mark or later, again depending on circumstances.

The reward is partly due to the fact that the correct investments have been made in customer lock-on, giving the enterprise the brand power to attract still other customers into the fold. Then enterprises, younger and more established, can begin to work by the same principle: project and get revenues from meaningful customer life expectancy, thanks to the longevity, breadth, depth and diversity of their spend. This eventually leaves the more staid organizations behind, still battling over monthly, quarterly and annual sales quotas.

The size of the investments that reap benefits over time may be quite considerable. Take Bezos, who deliberately initially over-invested in technology, customer acquisition and branding, and fulfilment (warehousing and logistics),[71] forfeiting profit as a result, in order to give customers a fully joined-up experience, after which the accumulated power created for Amazon could be leveraged to amass positive returns.

At the other extreme, these investments could be quite rudimentary, as in 2003 when Amazon discounted a much-awaited *Harry Potter* book by 40 per cent, by which stage the company's momentum had, of course, already gained considerable magnitude. There was even more to be had: pre-sales hit a million copies, of which 250,000 gushed from buyers who had never before made a purchase from Amazon.

Most traditional booksellers also discounted the book to attract customers into their stores. There was one important difference, nevertheless: they saw the book as a classic loss leader to get people to buy more books, or more *Harry Potter* books from them there and then. In contrast, Amazon's aim was to use these books (which, if stacked one on top of the other, would be more than twice the height of Mount Everest, the world's highest peak!)[72] to get customers on site so that it could to get to know them. Here was a very cost-effective way of making an investment (not a sales promotion) to get customers on board, an opportunity that would pay off in the long term (not just for the moment).

All of this is to say what's worth repeating: investments to gather and sustain momentum come from a state of mind that is quite different from the quick-win tactics of the product approach.

The Tangible Value of Intangibles

Amazon is a classic role model since it demonstrates the alternative customer approach, not because it is primarily (albeit not solely) internet-based. Generally, the investments that create customer currency are much more than only the combination of technology and marketing, and also include such relational and intellectual intangibles as skills, information, knowledge, expertise and partnering.

It is these that go to creating the highly interactive environments used by institutions that have successfully embraced and implemented the customer approach. When these investments are not simply made across the board but are dedicated to customers, they can bring about the momentum that produces the rewards. Says an executive from IBM: 'We can see a clear correlation between investments that are lined up behind specific business values for a customer and revenues rather than those that we make across the board. If these investments are made in order to give customers a specific outcome then the returns we get are not only larger, but more predictable.'

Yet ironically, these intangibles are the very assets that are often referred to as the non-sales or non-financial drivers – as opposed to the traditional, tangible assets and capital, which might get all the attention but aren't really the productive ingredients needed for giving and getting true, long-term customer value.[73]

Investing in these intangibles doesn't come easily to conventional players. They still prefer to put their money behind the tangibles, the assumed sales or financial drivers in which they have more faith – from plastic cards to new buildings, more sales representatives to new acquisitions. The reason is that they are regarded as more measurable and less subjective than the intangibles. They may also show returns more quickly, although these are quick to dissipate.

If they are still immersed in the old product model and lacking the new principles that can help them make and drive customer focus decisions, executives simply don't spend enough time thinking about how to use a combination of the intangibles to produce value for customers and wealth for the enterprise.[74] Either they can't make the connection between such assets and growth and performance, or they simply refuse to make a commitment because they are still trapped by short-term thinking and rewards, including their own bonuses, some commentators say, which are still linked to quarterly sales figures.

This all runs in the face of history, which has consistently reminded us that having these tangible assets and investments on a balance sheet is no sure indicator of long-term growth, or even of sustainable performance.[75] More recently, we have also seen that not having intangibles as an integral element in financial information can seriously affect the rate at which an enterprise changes.[76]

Importantly, by ignoring or underestimating the intangibles and their significance on performance, or hiding behind 'lag' accounting, what such executives and their enterprises miss out on is the platform from which to lever rewards *over time*. This can hold their enterprises back from what they need if they are to continue to go forward and step up their growth potential.

Good Reasons to Take Intangibles Seriously

Investments in intangibles pay because they provide the potential for exponential rewards. To see why, let's summarize their unique attributes:

First and most obvious is that since intangibles are abundant, they can be used over and over again. So instead of losing in value, as happens to tangibles that suffer wear and tear and depreciation, intangibles appreciate in value or enjoy positive depreciation the more they are used.

Second, once the investment is made in these intangibles, not only do they last longer and grow in the process, but the cost of using them decreases, so marginal expense to serve customers decreases and can even approximate zero.

Third, since these assets are also expandable – investments in technological infrastructures or databases, for instance – the initial outlay becomes no more than a baseline cost, requiring occasional refreshment and update. It involves none of the expensive replacements that traditional investments need, like more buildings, more stores, more factories or more oil rigs, all of which bring diminishing returns and eventually have to be acquired all over again, only to bring more diminishing returns.

Fourth, while traditional types of hard assets do make conventionalists feel safe and do appear to bolster their balance sheets, they don't actually drive the much-needed increased customer spend, whereas the intangibles that can produce personalized ongoing value do.

Fifth, intangible investments give the enterprise growth potential that comes from internal strength and capability extension, which it can continue to use, rather than from external sources. In all likelihood, with the latter the enterprise ends up expanding by doing or buying more of the same instead of building a platform for continued growth.

The sixth point is that these tangible assets have to be maintained from time to time. However, a better-looking store or a state of the art factory, machine or oil rig is hardly the way to ensure that customer spend is increasing and sustainable. In contrast, with the customer approach, the intangible levers are constantly being maintained and upgraded, on a monthly, daily, hourly or even minute-for-minute basis. If they are used correctly, they enhance the contact, dialogue, know-how, expertise and partnering network, enabling an enterprise to achieve ever-improved, joined-up customer experiences, with all the reward that these bring. The cost of all of this is minimal.

Finally, seventh on the list is the fact that intangible investments cost less than the capital investments required for traditional expansion. One official figure for retail is that investments in the kind of intangible assets we are talking about cost on average three times less per customer than do traditional investments.[77] This has the added effect of reducing the cost of capital, thus increasing the net present value of the customer base.

Reaping the Exponential Reward

Exhibit 16 shows the exponential curve that brings increased revenue and lower-cost rewards to the enterprise that gets to this stage, as it makes the breakthroughs to customer focus. Let's go through it in more detail.

Initially, there is a negative cash flow as the enterprise releases funds, which it must, and invests for perhaps months or years, depending on the circumstances, without revenues coming in. That's the bad news.

The good news is that once the initial investments are made up front and used for new ways of doing things to which customers start to respond positively, the bulk of the investment, because of its high

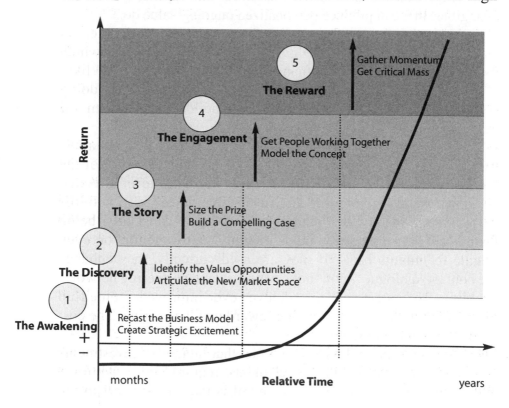

Exhibit 16 Conceptual exponential reward curve

intangible component, has been made and it only needs to be refreshed from time to time.

In addition, costs are offset by the knowledge gained through probing and questioning, getting and receiving feedback, used over and over again, constantly renewable at a cost of investment that, relatively speaking, amounts to next to nothing.

Further along in the curve, once there is a critical mass of take-up the enterprise begins to generate revenues. Concurrently it is also building a history on customers, and everyone in the organization has the benefit of the aggregated intelligence of the entire enterprise or extended network, so that the economies of skill (knowledge recycled) as well as the economies of sweep (people e-linked getting personalized services *en masse*) kick in to pull costs down.

It is now that the enterprise is not merely able to respond, it also can anticipate, reinforcing the customer 'lock-on' loop. By using the accumulated intelligence and deeply formed relationships and brand power, it can also diversify customers' spend, generating more growth by taking them into new market spaces.

Revenues go up because the brand and new way of doing things become contagious to a larger audience and the customer lock-on becomes self-sustaining. But as this happens, costs go down as a result of economies of stretch (taking the brand further afield at no or low extra cost), as Virgin has done with its brands, and economies of spread (enabling original and ongoing investments to be amortized over longer periods and more customers and geographies), as Amazon has done, repeating its experience in technology for merchants who want to go on-line, or again as Virgin has done in entering the Australian and US markets and making an impact – and profit – in record time in the travel and mobile communication sectors.

Quite apart from this, costs may also be pulled down further because the more the enterprise can anticipate, the more efficient it can be in the utilization of its resources, suppliers and employees.

In addition, partners are able to complement the delivery process that much more effectively. As the extended enterprise grows and resources, systems and information are shared, expenses can decline still further.

The result of all this for the transforming enterprise? Remarkably simple and powerful: as momentum builds, there is real potential for exponential rewards.

Taking Time Out

In many quarters a different outlook on time is becoming apparent, with executives adamant that they are rebuilding their enterprises for the long term, not merely month for month. Some organizations are simply refusing to hand over short-term financial projections, explaining that they detract from a more meaningful focus on the long term, while attracting the kinds of investors who only think short-term, like day traders or gamblers.[78]

In general, it seems that on the financial community front, institutions are becoming more patient as they see that the new customer-focused models consistently beat the old approach. 'They know anyone can do what it has always done, and they want to see a different way of making money, more creative and enduring.'

To make their assessments, instead of simply looking at today's share price and the organization's share capitalization, they are beginning to demand answers to a different set of questions, such as:

- What are you investing in?
- How many customers do you have?
- How does that translate into value for the enterprise in the future?

Investors, boards, banks, directors, journalists, theorists, big-name organizations and others all have a role to play in influencing this shift. But at the end of the day it is the enterprises making the groundbreaking differences in the marketplace that must take the lead in adjusting their mental and financial time frames so they can better reflect an ability to generate real and ongoing growth, by making and then leveraging their investments in customers.

Take Lexis Nexis US Corporate and Federal Market Division. Previously, the huge investments in infrastructure, databases and partnering needed to get from content to customer would have been near impossible to get through the system, since such investments were expected to show returns in the normal, short time frame. However, when the customer focus implementation was started, a three to five year view was taken and, importantly, the decision was communicated to investor communities, including the fact that margins on core items would have to take a knock initially, even though it would be more than compensated for.

This was accompanied by an explanation of how this all fitted together with the story, what new direction the division was taking, why, how and:

- how long it would take to get the rewards
- how the enterprise would perform better than in previous years
- how it would do better than its competitors because of the investments
- how the advantage reaped would be sustainable.

Outpacing Through Know-How

Another contributor to getting the promised reward, once momentum has gathered steam, is the fact that knowledge, the main ingredient in customer value, will work not only to help produce exponential returns, but also to keep the enterprise irretrievably ahead of competitors.

First, the enterprise gets ahead by using knowledge to make itself indispensable to individuals. Then, it uses it to grow and move up the curve at a steady clip. Finally, it uses its know-how to stay ahead of the game it may itself have conceived, making sure that the gap between the enterprise and potential rivals continues to widen as the enterprise learns and applies that learning faster than anyone else.

This is especially effective, as Gary Hamel points out, when the knowledge is complex, or if it is not easy to codify because it emanates from the fusion of several disciplines and people, which makes it difficult for others to copy.[79]

Using knowledge to get ahead in this way cannot happen with discrete products and services – even the most elaborate. Think about it: GE Imaging has sophisticated scanning hardware, but doctors still have to detect and analyse the problems. How does GE Imaging stay ahead? There is only one way.

It uses and updates its know-how to help in the analysis of the scanning, so that the machine or doctors can detect diseases earlier, diagnose more accurately to prevent or prolong the onset of the disease, and so enhance the speed and success of recovery.

GE Imaging – or anyone else for that matter – may have the tangible assets to update the hardware every few years and even cause huge disruptive technology waves in the process, but eventually some manufacturer will be on the offensive, ready to catch up. Enter knowledge as the centrepiece. Once the investment in the information system has been made, the enterprise can work with ever more minute items of information on a disease, continuously improving its analysis capability. That is how it keeps itself from being supplanted.

Leading by Knowing

So it is leading by knowing that keeps customers locked on and rivals locked out. When knowledge capital is explicitly linked to individual customers and constantly updated, it can't be easily commoditized by competitors. It then becomes an asset, potent enough to enable the organization to gather momentum and hold its ground, keeping others from invading its market space.

To get the resulting happy returns, top of mind for the transforming enterprise therefore must always be not 'Do we have or possess or own "it"?' but rather 'Did we get it?' and 'Do we understand how to do it?' and 'Are we using, reusing and updating our knowledge?'

From this will come a lead in the following ways.

More markets more quickly

What better way to stop others from jumping onto the bandwagon than blocking them before they even have a chance to get close? Knowledge, once accumulated, makes this possible, because it can be easily and cheaply adapted to move the enterprise quickly into new markets.

Given Amazon's well-earned skill base in technology, most other companies would keep it a secret and simply send merchants more and more visitors from its site or provide links in exchange for a commission. Why would it decide instead to share the technology with retail merchants, even competitors like Borders?

The answer is this: staying ahead with customers means making it too difficult for others to enter or offer an alternative.

Amazon Services Inc., a new division, uses its considerable skill to bolster revenues at next to no cost, by building merchants their own branded sites so that they can use the internet as a sales channel. So far this initiative has proved so successful that, as one commentator put it, even if Amazon never sells another book, it is still assured of a steady revenue stream.[80]

It is also worth noting that this is Amazon's way of keeping itself on top in the retail e-game, leveraging its learning in its ever smarter technology and knowledge to position itself as the leader, one step ahead. Why let anyone else in when what is earned can be used to keep them out?

By the same token, knowledge can be used to move into new geographies. This is the formula that has arguably been used by Direct Line, which started from scratch in the UK and now has over 5 million customers there as well as in Germany, Italy, Japan and Spain with whom it does business over the phone and on the internet. It is also how Virgin's Richard Branson has so swiftly and successfully swooped across the world. When growth is achieved in this way, the added spin-off is that the need for additional capital to expand is minimized.

Low-fares airline Virgin Blue's debut in Australia is only one instance of how the enterprise has established itself and become a dominant player within a short space of time, using knowledge as its capital. Virgin's investment there cost a mere £5 million!

Becoming the expert

Being and being seen as the expert is critical to gathering enough momentum to stay ahead, no matter what the size of the enterprise.

Take IBM: its specialist researchers and consultants prepare views on what will happen to technology in the coming years, and how it will affect every single market the company is in. As each trend evolves, these specialists go deeper and deeper into the issues, assessing their impact on organizations and their use of technology – say, risk compliance and regulation in the financial market sector. These impacts are fed into all elements of the business that serve customers, so that people know and can embed this knowledge into their part of the offering in a proactive way.

Even for small start-ups, becoming the expert in their chosen market space is an essential feature of keeping the momentum going to get and stay ahead. Of its own accord, at the cusp of showing its first profits, Webstar Healthcare – 'never wanting anyone to think about pharmacy medicine management without thinking of us first' – embarked on research to establish how well PCTs were doing in the new pharmacy reform initiative in the UK. Of the 330 PCTs, 203 participated, enough for the enterprise to build up a comparative database and use it for benchmarking purposes.

Now more have joined and the Department of Health has commissioned yet more work from the now not-so-new start-up, which has positioned itself as the authoritative voice in the new market space, thereby enticing more PCTs into the project to build even more momentum by accumulating more knowledge, reputation and brand positioning.

Massifying the knowledge

Part of the trick of staying ahead is to capture knowledge gleaned from the behaviour unique to an individual customer, consolidate the findings and transfer the relevant bits to other customers – when, where and how they need them.

For instance, Lexis Nexis conscientiously and continuously observes the behaviour of customers such as sales departments, financial managers or scientists, tracking how users link information in their decision-making processes. It then takes these connections and aggregates the components into new value adds, making them mainstream for other customers.

Through a never-ending flow of improvements, it captures the real-time interactive opportunity. The net effect of this is that it can continuously produce superior value at low delivered cost, thus setting up protective barriers to any predators who may be waiting in the wings.

Creating next practice

Hand in hand with becoming the expert is that an enterprise creates next practice by virtue of constantly updating its best practice. An example: since embracing customer focus for its various multifaceted activities, Baxter Healthcare has maintained its lead as the acclaimed standard, by collecting knowledge gained in the field and turning it into added value. It actively seeks out in minute detail:

- What country is getting the best results?
- What region in this country is getting the best results?
- What physician/nurse within the region is getting the best results?

Then a template is created of exactly what is done, how, when in the intervention process, how often and for what kinds of patients. From this the best demonstrated practice is written up, disseminated across the enterprise and constantly updated to become next practice.

Using knowledge in the ways described in fact presents an enterprise with a strange contradiction. On the one hand, the more complex and difficult the knowledge is to capture and record, and the more it is geared to the distinct value of an individual customer, the more likely it is that it will help to keep rivals out. On the other hand, to generate momentum from the benefits of reusing knowledge means making it, or parts of it, as standardized as possible, so that it can be spread and used, constantly adapted to suit the needs of individuals.

When such knowledge comes from unique experiences with customers and resides in people's heads, appropriate systems need to be in place to motivate these people to share their experiences so that the entire knowledge base can be continually elevated, and each person's capability when dealing with a customer can ascend to that collective whole.

Ideally, this means that the people interacting with customers need to be encouraged and rewarded for bringing knowledge back to the enterprise all the time. At IBM, for instance, consultants are expected to consciously look for what is replicable, and then record it in a global database so that others can use and refine it. Their contribution is weighted in their appraisals, to ensure an ongoing flow of knowledge that executives believe keeps the enterprise ahead in environments that are changing at lightning speed.

Measuring and Communicating Success

For an enterprise to usher in the new rewards of customer focus, the correct things have to be both measured and communicated.

Once the metrics reflect where the prize comes from and how it is attained, the ultimate breakthrough will have been made. It is at this point that people, internal and external, will be able to make the connections between:

- what has been done to advance the customer approach
- what has been spent
- how this is linked to performance drivers
- how it is linked to growth and financial success.

As we have indicated before, it is no secret that current accounting and financial practice and instruments are hopelessly out of date for a world in which customers are the focal point of value. Customers are what must be managed, and what brings value to them must be measured.[81]

The present system simply cannot account for when:

- value is infinite, not finite
- labour is brains, not bodies
- raw material is abundant, not scarce.

Research also tells us that currently it is not unusual for different silos or business units within the same enterprise to use entirely different methodologies to measure performance. This is clearly a symptom of a culture where each part continues to work in a different direction (even against each other), instead of being unified under one powerful and superordinate customer concept.[82]

Not all Financial Data are Created Equal

In truth, there is all-round and growing recognition by scholars, investors and executives alike that conventional instruments are not good or sufficient on their own to reflect the strength and ability of an enterprise to create and extract future wealth. Current accounting practices may make the numbers reliable and, as Thomas Stewart puts it, it is no small thing that they make fraud difficult.[83] Nevertheless, reliability is no substitute for relevance, especially if future growth has to be sacrificed.

Proposed changes to traditional financials to reflect progress and success include acknowledging the kinds of expenses that should be legitimately capitalized, since they will provide the springboard for growth in the years to follow; agreement that more disclosure is needed so that the new story can unfold and be sold; and working with new and old accounting statements in tandem and being able to cope with that ambiguity.

Widespread concern from legislators and policy makers in the United States, the European Union and among members of the OECD has resulted in increasing efforts to take up the not insignificant challenge of how to incorporate non-financial (intangible) data into financial statements. This is all in the spirit of being able to present a more realistic picture of good or poor decision making and decision makers.

For example, the US Securities and Exchange Commission and the Financial Accounting Standards Board now recommend that in addition to the usual financial statements, enterprises should publish supplementary information on their new business models. In particular, more emphasis has to be given to the intangibles accumulated through investment, like customer relations, innovation capabilities, new staff skills, customer R&D and so on, all of which may be non-material but contribute to building the material value.[84]

Cashflow Analysis: Connecting Customer Focus to Growth

This growing awareness that old accounting principles and metrics are inadequate has shifted the emphasis from simply looking at balance sheets and profit and loss (P&L) accounts to cash flows. That links in more suitably with customer focus, and with how to measure and communicate the rewards brought to those who have made the brave moves to transform enterprises and industries.

Fortunately, executives are aided and abetted by new technologies. Thanks to them, the data-gathering burden that was almost
impossible to do thoroughly in the past is now entirely feasible.
Added to that is the fact that the cost of this technology is continuing to fall.

If we look more closely and compare traditional balance sheet
and P&L accounts to cash flows, we quickly see the relevance of
cashflow analysis (see Table 10.1).

We begin with the fact that old financial accounts are a snapshot
of how the enterprise stands today. In contrast, the whole point of
the customer-focus transformation is to perpetuate the flow of
giving and getting customer value over time, by capturing the
major proportion of spend in the chosen market space, expressed in
a statement of the prize over the contemplated years.

Cash flow encapsulates net present value (NPV), which provides
an assessment of what the future value of the customer base is
today, given certain actions. It also indicates what cash will be
freed over and above what is required to make the customer focus
initiative work.

Cashflow analysis has the added advantage that it invites the
much-needed high-ground discussions by boards, executives,
investors and journalists who influence the public at large, on what
exactly it is that is driving the performance today and for the
future. This makes the connection between customer focus and
growth.

Table 10.1 Traditional accounting and cashflow analysis

Balance sheets and P&L accounts	Cash flows
Show financial standing of enterprise today	Show potential for customer value in the future
Show profits, assets and liabilities at current scale	Say how cash could be used to grow the business
Look at tangibles almost exclusively	Look at intangibles as well
Used to assess past performance	Track ongoing performance
Identify financial health of silos within the organization	Tell overall story of how well the total organization is doing
Encourage short-term behaviour	Drive the longer term

Then comes the fact that what matters is the *meaning* behind the metrics. The balance sheet and P&L can't provide this, certainly not if considered exclusively on their own.

How much the organization sold this year, for instance, says absolutely nothing about its prospects for the next. Profit does say how well an enterprise did and is doing today at covering its expenses to earn revenues. However, cost of goods sold, which is the most important component of the equation, is first a function of what is expensed when, and second may not even be a meaningful number for enterprises that live in the intangible world of customer value.

Also the old measures are horribly static, representations that gear attention to what can be done with the current capacity and scale. In contrast, looking at cash flow tells executives how the enterprise transforming to customer focus has been doing, or could be doing, in using its cash to grow the business.

Add to this the fact that balance sheets may look rich and fabulous, but may in no way contain the assets that will bring the enterprise from a product focus to a customer focus, or that will sustain its growth into the future. What does appear on the balance sheet could be good, bad or neutral, today or tomorrow, depending on all sorts of developments or disruptions that the enterprise could either wait for or itself decide to make happen.

In contrast, what does *not* appear on that balance sheet is probably what has produced the value, and it is this that needs to be tracked.

So the next point is that the intangibles that should be put to work and linked to the performance drivers and financial results are not on the balance sheets – yet. Nevertheless, although they are ignored in conventional accounts and valuations, they are embedded in or can be extracted from cash flows, where their effects can be seen, felt and discussed.

The bottom line, so to speak, on cash flow is that it fills out the picture and is transparent about what matters. It provides executives with insight and opens up avenues for discussing where the money was spent and whether the decisions taken were good or bad, in as much as they have yielded and are likely to continue to yield the economic returns from customer value by way of increased revenues and decreased costs, over an extended time-span.

When they understand this difference, executives are better placed to evaluate the decisions made to date and line up resources for investments that will continue to bring the long-run returns they want.

Instead of terminating initiatives that may require more time or making pronouncements about cutting costs across the board to bolster profits quickly – which may sound naïve but happens all the time, often to the detriment of customer value – boards and executives are more likely to be able to see what actually created the value and what didn't. They will therefore know what to keep and what to cut.

Cash flows are meant to illuminate how the enterprise has used its resources to shift its market position, and what returns are likely to be coming in over time and at what cost. The good thing about them is that they track financial health and decisions over time instead of simply homing in on a moment in time. That makes it difficult for the powers that be to ignore three important factors:

- where the enterprise began
- how far it has come
- where it is headed.

Another deficiency in conventional accounting tools is the same old problem of silo transactional mentality being perpetuated. When the numbers aggregate up the bits into one metric, it says nothing about whether the organization is strong enough to enter the future. When each bit is examined separately, it gives no clue as to how individual silos may have contributed to overall customer value, nor how well the total enterprise is doing by putting together its energy and resources to produce real value.

This further tempts and encourages short-term behaviour and poor decisions in all layers of the organization.

Put all of this together and it is easy to see that the practices and instruments used to measure and communicate success can either herald in the new customer era for all time and be the engine for continued momentum and growth – or they can hold it back.

Leading Questions

It is now well known that in addition to the obvious problems, traditional accounting is notoriously retroactive. That is, it is not exactly conducive to making the breakthroughs that the forward-thrusting enterprise has to accomplish to reinvent itself and the future.

Not only is the fixation on the past out of sync with the thinking and actions that take an enterprise along a growth trajectory, it can also be dangerously misleading, and in the worst case can result in outright failure.

That is why, much to the astonishment of everyone concerned, six months after it reported its best profits in history (£1.2 billion) and the very year it had enjoyed the highest return on sales of any European retailer, M&S's sales plummeted and its profits plunged.

Box 10.1 Leading questions

1   Has the enterprise unveiled an exciting view about the future and told a compelling story?

2   Does this create new opportunities for wealth, demand new names to describe what has been done and change the way the industry operates?

3   Have investments been made to get customer 'lock on'?

4   Are executives managing the pace?

5   Have well-known partners/developers joined in?

6   Is a platform being built with future leverage potential for early or substantial results?

7   Is the brand becoming increasingly infectious to customers?

8   Do cash flows reveal future potential for maximizing share of customer spend?

9   Has what is being done reflected well on the relevant performance measures, including financials?

10 Has the enterprise found a new way of dealing with customers that has potential for continual renewal?

It is also why exactly the same thing happened to IBM when it went from making US$6 billion in 1990 to losing US$8 billion in 1993, having had a record share price only six months before the crash.

Yes, an enterprise must account for its recent performance and operational efficiency. But equally, it must be able to demonstrate that it can prosper tomorrow by virtue of the moves it is making today.

This is what investors, boards, the public and executives need to know – and are increasingly demanding.

So in the end, the true mark of success depends on the answers to the questions in Box 10.1.

Moving Forward

Once there is a commitment to customer focus, the enterprise enters a challenging period of 18 months to 3 years, which can even carry over into 5 years if the enterprise starts from scratch or is in deep crisis.

This is not without good reason: true customer focus requires profound change to the way the organization or industry operates, if it is not only to deliver the substantial rewards, but make them long-lasting.

Leaders need to be prepared to take people through a systematic process with the five phases and ten breakthrough points we have described, none of which can operate in isolation and all of which are interwoven and reiterative, despite the seemingly disciplined and orderly approach. It is ultimately their faith and passion, consistency and persistence that drive the implementation process forward so that, in the end, customer focus takes on a life of its own. Leaders need to use an intricate combination of discipline and discovery, creativity and structure, emotional and rational appeal to make it work and anchor all actions in customers with a concept and story 'which people can't ignore because it's just so obviously the right way to go'.

The moment the need for change is stated in a way that inspires people to feel and think differently and to willingly break with history – even if it means deviating from what happens to be working right now – the enterprise enters a new era in its existence and the implementation has begun.

As the milestones go by, the language and concepts become commonplace and, more importantly, the customer ethos that dictates what gets done, where and why finally gets deep into the essence of the enterprise – into what it is, what it does and what it prides itself on. It is then that the customer approach becomes rooted in behaviour, shaping all subsequent priorities and actions both internally and in the marketplace.

The principles and template we have discussed hold for all enterprises, private and public. However, each and every enterprise will have to decide how to apply the customer approach to its own specific environment to make the growth connection. Some, operating in relatively staid situations, can move more slowly; those in lightning-speed environments will have to work at a much more rapid pace. Some will struggle to open minds and doors; others will have an easier time of it. Some will find that the model fits as it is; others will have to adapt it.

What Goes Round Can Stick

Regardless of its unique situation, each enterprise will find that, once it has successfully transformed itself, it becomes resilient[85] enough to constantly and easily renew itself, rather than having to enforce and undergo radical reconstructions in times of disruption and change, when it can least be afforded.

The successes that ensue from getting customer focus entrenched into the culture and making a permanent imprint will not only exist in the present, but can be repeated over and over again as the enterprise consciously and continuously refreshes itself in its quest for growth and success in unknowable futures that it may even have to invent.

However, that doesn't mean that efforts can stop – quite the opposite. The first time IBM went into a crisis, Lou Gerstner and his team breathed life back into it by going from just selling products to making services the heart of the business. Reborn, next time round IBM didn't wait for a crisis before it took the courageous actions needed to push the enterprise yet further forward. Hurt but not hindered by the fact that increasing the quantity and enhancing the quality of IT had not worked, but instead left companies frustrated and hopelessly out of pocket, IBM applied its remade power to try to help customers adapt to ever-changing circumstances.

If the new IBM provides customers with fresh insights and horizons, and with it computing on demand as easy as turning on a tap or a light switch, to give them the systems they need to excel in the marketplaces of the future, it will have remade itself – yet again.

That's the ultimate object of enduring customer focus.

Simply pumping more money into an old model that no longer works won't provide any organization with growth, or help it regain lost ground. Whatever the future holds for IBM or any of the examples discussed in this book – or for all of us – what any enterprise needs is a model that is robust enough to enable it to continue to rejuvenate itself, regardless of the situation. This means that it can be part of, and indeed create, an illustrious future.

The customer-focused approach is such a model, because instead of rendering irrelevant what the enterprise does and may even do well when everything changes, it becomes the driver. Enterprises become programmed to creatively and constantly take new innovations – either their own or those of others – and incorporate them into their offerings. That is the only way to create the kind of long-lasting customer value and indispensability that will optimize their spend over time.

What other option is there? The old models and initiatives, even the expensive ones, are no longer working.

For those of you just about to take up the challenge and begin the breakthrough steps to customer focus, Table 10.2 provides summary guidelines to help you on your way.

Table 10.2 Summary guideline sheet

Phase	Breakthrough	You know you have made it when:	Actions needed to get there include:	Implementation is driven forward because this:
1 AWAKENING	Create Strategic Excitement	Enough of the correct people see and feel the urgent need to change	• Set new direction • Communicate risks & opportunities • Demystify numbers and dangers • Work through 'points of light'	* Triggers excitement & enthusiasm * Raises level of consciousness * Gets both rational and emotional appeal * Instils passion & positive energy
AWAKENING	Recast the Business Model	There is understanding on why and how the customer model is different and more relevant	• Provide forum at high level • Embed principles as stimulators & guidelines for decision making • Show connection of new principles to growth & performance	• Encourages new ground to be explored jointly • Aligns perspectives & spirit • Builds a common language and set of principles and tools
2 DISCOVERY	Articulate the New Market Space	Agreement is reached on how far to extend aspirations & boundaries	• Frame new competitive arena around customer outcome • Express market space across company • Use research to substantiate hypothesis	• Makes the direction concrete and easy to communicate • Influences through involvement • Turns positive feelings to action
DISCOVERY	Identify the Value Opportunities	People uncover specific values that become the potential for new wealth creation	• Choose key markets • Use the customer activity cycle as organizing tool • Uncover gaps through unified customer experience • Define new value add opportunities • Show role of silos	• The structured methodology boosts confidence & credibility • Takes ideas from the abstract to concrete • Fosters both creativity and imagination • Packages unified customer concept • Builds traction which accelerates take-up.
3 STORY	Build a Compelling Case	A story unfolds and is told and sold around customers, and what needs to change	• Build enterprise wide picture around customer outcome • Mirror this in a new core purpose • Identify needed initiatives and projects	• Makes visual & cognitive impact • Embeds language & concepts in culture • Allows people to see where they fit • Gives the customer approach more meaning and relevance
STORY	Size The Prize	The numbers reveal growth and returns big enough to warrant the investment	• Motivate investment made on customer time value • Calculate total customer value on revenues up and costs down	• Stimulates confidence & trust • Attracts resources & budget • Lines up thinking and investments behind customer value
4 ENGAGEMENT	Model the Concept	Customers validate the concept and values and buy into getting it right	• Select relevant customers • Test and refine work to date including new value opportunities • Choose hot spots as entry points • Get proof of concept and early wins	• Provides the testimony which leads to heightened credibility & energy • Gets customers to influence others • Profiles successes that bolsters buy-in
ENGAGEMENT	Get People Working Together	Silos and partners start to work jointly becoming actively involved	• Involve silos & partners in development and delivery • Deploy best resources • Demonstrate gains all round • Showcase & celebrate victories	• Makes silos work to same goals • Turns motivation to commitment • Grows familiarity & use of concepts • Develops new expertise & skills • Enhances customer experience and value
5 REWARD	Get Critical Mass	There is compounding take up as the brand becomes contagious	• Gain brand credibility • Invest in customer education • Manage 'push/pull' energy rhythm to draw people in at right time	• Converts insiders & outsiders • Gets more partners/developers to join • Compounds demand
REWARD	Gather Momentum	Rewards begin to be reaped with visible success and a lead that is sustainable	• Articulate rewards • Use cashflow analysis to show progress and successes • Factor in intangible gains • Leverage know-how to stay ahead	• Makes new concept the new standard • Shows connection between customer growth & performance • Hails & reinforces customer approach • Attracts more investment allocation

REFERENCES

1 Quote comes from article by S. Dubner, 'Calculating the Irrational in Economics', *New York Times*, 28 June 2003.

2 For examples of the importance of customer, and not product, focus on growth and profitability, see: G. Day, 'Creating a Superior Customer Relating Capability', *MIT Sloan Management Review*, Spring 2003; W. Reinartz and V. Kumar, 'The Impact of Customer Relationship Characteristics on Profitable Lifetime Duration', *Journal of Marketing*, Vol. 67, 2003.

3 The limits to growth by constantly churning out ever more products and services has been discussed by, amongst others, A. Slywotzky and R. Wise, 'The Growth Crisis-And How to Escape It', *Harvard Business Review*, July 2002; M. Vandenbosch and N. Dawar, 'Beyond Better Products: Capturing Value in Customer Interactions', *MIT Sloan Management Review*, Summer 2002.

4 Amongst the copious literature on the fact that a huge proportion of mergers fail, and why, see for example: K. Donahue, 'How To Ruin a Merger: Five People Management Pitfalls to Avoid', *Harvard Management Update*, 2001; L. Seldon and G. Colvin, 'M&A Needn't Be a Loser's Game', *Harvard Business Review*, June 2003; and P. Ghemawat and F. Ghadar, 'The Dubious Logic of Global Megamergers', *Harvard Business Review*, July–August 2000. For research on shareholders often being worse off with mergers and acquisitions see N. Deogun and S. Lipin, 'Cautionary Tales: When Big Deals Turn Bad', *Wall Street Journal*, 8 December 1999.

5 The Harvard case referred to on Marks & Spencer's performance is by J. Bower and J. Matthews, 'Marks & Spencer: Sir Richard Greenbury's Quiet Revolution', *Harvard Business School Case Study*, 1995. For more, see also J. Bevan, *The Rise and Fall of Marks & Spencer*, Profile Books, London, 2001.

6 A. Hall, for IBM quote in 'Curing a Sickness Called Success', *Sunday Times*, 15 December 2002.

7 Airline catering statements come from an industry survey by SITA, 'A Farewell to In-Flight Catering', *International Herald Tribune*, 14 March 2003.

8 S. Spreir and D. Sherman, for the research on admired companies and long-term goals, based on six years of research by the Hay Group of

Consultants and reported in *Fortune*, 'Staying Ahead of the Curve', 3 March 2003.

9 For more on the Boots example, see: Final Results for 2002, The Boots Company, plc: Earnings Presentation, Fair Disclosure Wire Service, 5 June 2003; 'Boots Adapts to Changing Consumer', *Chain Drug Review*, 16 December 2002; and N. Cope, 'Boots Ditches Well-being Strategy to Return to its Roots as a Chemist', *Independent*, 28 March 2003.

10 J. Glassman, on investors' view of Amazon, quoted from 'Why Amazon.com's Short Term Losses May Hide Long Term Success', *International Herald Tribune*, 10 July 2000.

11 Bezos quotes from: C. Bayers, 'The Last Laugh', *Business 2.0*, September 2002; S. Hansell, 'A Front Row Seat as Amazon Gets Serious', *New York Times*, 20 May 2001.

12 R. Kanter and 'knee jerk' reactions in 'Strategy as Improvisation Theory', *Sloan Management Review*, Winter 2002.

13 For more on people who are energizers, and the characteristics and virtues of these people, see R. Cross, W. Baker and A. Parker, 'What Creates Energy In Organizations?' in *Sloan Management Review*, Summer 2003.

14 Figures for Japan and health care come from D. Pilling, 'Over-prescribing Adds $3.5bn to Drugs Bill', *Financial Times*, 27 May 2003.

15 Frederick Reichheld made this point in his article, 'The One Number You Need to Grow', *Harvard Business Review*, December 2003.

16 J. Cigliano, M. Georgiadis, D. Pleasance and S. Whalley, for research on why loyalty hasn't worked: 'The Price of Loyalty', *McKinsey Quarterly*, 2000. For interesting reading on this theme see also G. Dowling, 'Customer Relationship Management: In B2C Markets Often Less Is More', *California Management Review*, Spring 2002.

17 K. Reinartz, for loyalty not bringing about the increases companies are after, in 'The Mismanagement of Customer Loyalty', *Harvard Business Review*, July 2002.

18 Quote is from F. Reichheld and D. Rigby, in 'Avoid the Four Perils of CRM', *Harvard Business Review*, July–August 2000.

19 P. Molineux, for data on loyalty, CRM, banking spend, and results in the UK: 'CRM: What Went Wrong?' *Financial Services*, 1 July 2002.

20 McKinsey research from J. Cigliano, M. Georgiadis, D. Pleasance and S. Whalley, 'The Power of Loyalty: Creating Winning Retail Loyalty Programs', *McKinsey Research in Marketing*, 2000.

21 N. Cicutti for stats on two-thirds and 2 per cent loyalty from 'Account Holders Have No Loyalty to Banks', *Financial Times*, 30 April 2002.

22 Bezos quote from R. Hof, 'Amazon.com: The Wild World of E-Commerce', *Business Week,* 14 December 1998.

23 Amazon customer satisfaction scores based on ACSI scores, from Amazon.com press release, 'Amazon.com Launches Amazon Services Subsidiary to Connect Retailers to the Web's Leading E-Comm', 10 June 2003.

24 Amazon customers spending 10 per cent more comes from a Forrester Research figure, reported in M. Behr, 'CIO Insight: Will Amazon.com's Growth Strategy Work?' *E-Week,* 4 December 2003.

25 R. Lieber, 'An On-the-Job Hazard: The Corporate Travel Office', *Wall Street Journal,* 25 June 2003.

26 For more on market spaces and development of concept, see S. Vandermerwe's work, in chronological order: 'New Competitive Spaces: Jointly Investing in New Customer Logic,' *Columbia Journal of World Business,* 31 (Winter 1996); *The 11th Commandment: Transforming to 'Own' Customers,* John Wiley, London, 1996; *Customer Capitalism: Getting Increasing Returns in New Market Spaces,* Nicholas Brealey, London, 1999 (republished by Whurr Publishers, London, 2001); 'How Increasing Value to Customers Improves Business Results', *Sloan Management Review,* Fall 2000.

27 P. Maraldo and E. Lister, for 10 per cent of spend in total healthcare market space, in 'Reframing the Industry', *Pharmaceutical Executive,* Vol. 22, issue 9, September 2002.

28 See 'The New Blue', *Business Week,* 17 March 2003.

29 For more on IBM and research teams, see B. Schlender, 'How Big Blue Is Turning Geeks into Gold', *Fortune,* 9 June 2003.

30 The customer activity cycle methodology was first published by S Vandermerwe in 'Jumping into the Customer's Activity Cycle', *Columbia Journal of World Business,* Summer 1993; for more details see also *The 11th Commandment: Transforming to 'Own' Customers,* John Wiley, London, 1996; for more on gap analysis see S. Vandermerwe, *Customer Capitalism: Getting Increasing Returns in New Market Spaces,* Nicholas Brealey, London, 1999 (republished by Whurr Publishers, London, 2001).

31 A quarter of all relocations fail, as reported in *Resident Abroad,* July 2000, based on research done on UK firms by Cedent International Assignment Services, a US global relocation company.

32 Costs of relocation reported in *Resident Abroad,* July 2000, based on research done on UK firms by Cedent International Assignment Services, a US global relocation company. This is confirmed for US companies by research done by, for instance, B. Cheng, 'Home Truths

about Foreign Postings', *Business Week*, 15 July 2002; and R. Swaak, 'Too Many, Too Much Cost, Too Little Planning', Franklin E. Allen & Associates Consultants, 1997.

33 For statistics on the value of post-sales services, see P. Baumgartner and R. Wise, 'Go Downstream: The New Profit Imperative in Manufacturing', *Harvard Business Review*, September–October 1999; M. Dennis and A. Kambil, 'Services Management: Building Profits after the Sale', Accenture White Paper, 2003; and J. Wright and T. Pugh, 'The Changing Landscape for After-Sale Service', Frontline and Accenture Joint Publication, 3 July 2003.

34 For proverb, see M. Hattersley, 'The Managerial Art of Telling a Story', *Harvard Management Update*, January 1997.

35 M. Hattersley, 'The Management Art of Telling a Story', *Harvard Management Update*, 1997.

36 D. Kirkpatrick for quote on Gerstner and foils versus talk, from 'The Future of IBM: Lou Gerstner Seems to have Pulled off a Miracle', *Fortune*, 18 February 2002.

37 Health problems that can be predicted and prevented 70 per cent of the time and healthcare costs decreased by 50 per cent from 'Haelen Group Interview with CEO Julie Meek', *USA Today*, 21 January 2001.

38 Unilever from 'Boom Time for Domestic Help as More Consumers Become Service Junkies', M2 Press Wire, 25 September 2002; and S. Ellison, 'Myhome Cleans House for Busy Londoners', *Asian Wall Street Journal*, 14 June 2001.

39 *Brand Strategy*, for quote on Unilever post mortem, in 'Customer Life Made Easy', 4 November 2002.

40 Some of those who have the made the case for a change to the standard accounting principles to better incorporate intangibles include J. Daum, *Intangible Assets and Value Creation,* John Wiley, New York, 2003; and several works of Baruch Lev, for instance B. Lev and P. Zarowin, 'The Boundaries of Financial Reporting and How to Extend Them', *Journal of Accounting*, Vol. 37, no. 2, Autumn 1999.

41 For more on the debate and what can go wrong, see A. Berkowitz and R. Rampell, 'How to Hide Expenses via Accounting Gimmicks', Wall Street Journal Online, 3 October 2002; and P. Black, 'Mind the GAAP', *Registered Rep.*, 1 September 2002.

42 Quote from Baruch Lev is from 'Baruch Lev on Intangible Assets – An Interview by Alan Kay', *Knowledge Management*, 19 June 2001.

43 For more on the new algorithm, see S. Vandermerwe, 'How Increasing Value to Customers Improves Business Results', *Sloan Management Review*, Fall 2000.

44 P. Seybold, for Amazon evaluation, from 'Don't Count Out Amazon', *Business 2.0*, September 2000.

45 The Virgin brand and the UK pension scheme were noted in the Henley Centre's *Report on Trust and the Media*, 2001, done for the UK Radio Authority Board; the J. Walter Thompson finding on Virgin's brand potential was underscored in *Total Immersion Branding Beefs up Marketing Competitiveness: Companies Are Breaking New Ground in Enabling Consumers to 'Live the Brand'*, a study by Through-the-Loop Consulting Ltd., 1999, available on www.through theloop.com.

46 Unilever example from C. Prysty, 'Marketing – Unilever Raises its India Game: Squeezed by Growing Competition from Foreign and Domestic rivals, Anglo-Dutch Multinational Unilever is Diversifying from Just Mass-Producing Consumer Goods to Direct Sales and Value-Added Services', *Far Eastern Economic Review*, 30 October 2003.

47 R. Dhar and R. Glazer, for risk hedging and customers, 'Hedging Customers', *Harvard Business Review*, May 2003.

48 For different versions of how the lifetime present value of customers can be derived, see for instance R. Blattberg, G. Getz and J. Thomas, *Customer Equity: Building and Managing Relationships as Valuable Assets*, Harvard Business School Press, Cambridge, MA, 2001; E. Ofek, 'Customer Profitability and Lifetime Value', *Harvard Business School Note*, 7 August 2002; R. Rust, V. Zeithaml and K. Lemon, *Driving Customer Equity*, Free Press, New York, 2002.

49 Adapted from a quote by S. Jurvetson in G. Hamel, 'Bringing Silicon Valley Inside', *Harvard Business Review*, September–October 1999.

50 Research on corporate entrepreneurs who have undergone this sort of transformation supports the ability to sell ideas as the most important personal characteristic needed. See work by S. Vandermerwe and S. Birley, 'The Corporate Entrepreneur: Leading Organisational Transformation', *Long Range Planning*, June 1997.

51 For interesting fresh commentary on the importance of the emotional and the rational approaches in implementing change, see: H. Bruch and S. Ghoshal, 'Unleashing Organizational Energy', *Sloan Management Review*, Fall 2003; J. Kotter and D. Cohen, *The Heart of Change*, Harvard Business School Press, Cambridge, MA, 2002; and P. LaDuke, T. Andrews and K. Yamashita, 'Igniting a Passion for Innovation', *Harvard Strategy and Innovation Report*, July/August 2003.

52 The first edition of Everett Rogers' *The Diffusion of Innovation* was

publishcd in 1962. The most recent edition was published in 2003 by Simon & Schuster, New York.

53 Work by Gary Hamel corroborates the fact that to attract funds, new initiatives require more proof than do incremental moves. Reported in G. Hamel and L. Valikangas, 'The Quest for Resilience', *Harvard Business Review*, September 2003. Most of the examples are still product-related, however.

54 See work done by J. Mauzy and R. Harriman, reported in *Creativity, Inc.: Building an Inventive Organization*, Harvard Business School Press, Cambridge, MA, 2003.

55 For more on the initiative of using IBM as a role model, see 'The New Blue', *Business Week*, 17 March 2003.

56 G. Hamel, for capitalization data on Starbucks and Nestlé, 'Letters to the Editor: Revolution vs. Evolution – You Need Both', *Harvard Business Review*, May–June 2001.

57 V. Vishwanath and D. Harding, 'The Starbucks Effect', *Harvard Business Review*, March 2000.

58 For findings of research over the years on the problems of getting people to work together internally, see R. Cross, S. Borgatti and A. Parker, 'Making Invisible Work Visible: Using Social Network Analysis to Support Strategic Collaboration', *California Management Review*, Winter 2002.

59 See for instance J. Byrne and H. Timmons, 'Tough Times for a New CEO: How Ken Chenault of AmEx is Being Tested in Ways Few Could Have Imagined', *Business Week*, 29 October 2001, for *inter alia* American Express's competitive position vis-à-vis MasterCard and Visa.

60 US Government initiative and Pennsylvania data from S. Ballmer, 'The Promise of e-Government', *Outlook*, no. 1, 2002.

61 P. Drucker, 'The Next Society: A Survey of the Near Future', *The Economist*, 3 November 2001.

62 According to the survey entitled 'Collaborative Commerce: Compelling Benefits, Significant Obstacles', Nervewire, 2002, highly collaborative partners realize a 40 per cent increase in revenues versus the 12 per cent average increase that moderately collaborative partners get. The results were reported in a study from the IBM Institute for Business Value, by J. McKinley, M. Badgett, W. Connor and M. Bowen, 'Building Customer Relationships Through Indirect Channels', 2003.

63 Scaling through centralization can stunt employee development, limit opportunities for innovation, impede customer responsiveness and

numb sensitivity to environmental changes, say F. Pil and M. Holweg in 'Exploring Scale', *Sloan Management Review*, Winter, 2003.

64 Plans revealed by Virgin in 'Virgin Atlantic Airways'; www.luxury-travelsource.com, 2003.

65 F. Vogelstein, 'The Tao of Jeff', *Fortune*, 26 May 2003.

66 From 'Danish Lego Opens First Education Centre in Australia', *Danish News Digest*, 28 August 2003,

67 Customer resistance in Europe to genetically modified foods from J. Geary, 'Risky Business', *Time*, 28 July 2003.

68 J. Kotter and D. Cohen, *The Heart of Change*, Harvard Business School Press, Cambridge, MA, 2002.

69 Twenty per cent is a rule of thumb, although Rogers mentioned innovators and early adopters (people who take on innovations first) totalling about 16 per cent of a normal population. See E. Rogers, *The Diffusion of Innovation*, Simon & Schuster, New York, 2003.

70 For instance W. Chan and R. Mauborgne, in 'Tipping Point Leadership', *Harvard Business Review,* April 2003, used this classic well-known phenomenon to demonstrate how the New York City Transit Police transformed itself by getting its staff to become more aware and effective.

71 For more on Amazon.com's investments in technology, customer acquisition and branding, and fulfilment, see M. Stabingas, 'Building A World-Class Multichannel Customer Experience', *Forrester Consumer Forum Magazine*, September 2003, and his presentation 'The Evolution of Amazon.com' at Forrester Consumer Forum, September 2003.

72 *Harry Potter* figures from S. Hansell, 'Amazon Reduces its Quarterly Loss', *New York Times*, 23 July 2003.

73 The role of intangibles in the creation of customer value and as a driver of corporate performance, and how to account for these assets, has been discussed by, amongst others: J. Daum, *Intangible Assets and Value Creation*, John Wiley, London, 2003; J. Hand and B. Lev, *Intangible Assets: Values, Measures, Risks*, Oxford University Press, New York, 2003; and B. Lev, *Intangibles: Management, Measurement and Reporting*, Brookings Institute, Washington, 2001.

74 This is corroborated by research on organizations and growth by, *inter alia*, A. Slywotzky and R. Wise, 'The Growth Crisis – And How to Escape It', *Harvard Business Review*, July 2002.

75 See for example K. Funk, 'Sustainability and Performance', *Sloan Management Review*, Winter 2003.

76 Baruch Lev and Paul Zarowin made this point in 'The Boundaries of

Financial Reporting and How to Extend Them', *Journal of Accounting*, Vol. 37, no. 2 (Autumn 1999).

77 The cost data for retailers comes from a worldwide study by G. Sand and E. Jones, 'Keeping the Customer Profitably Satisfied', White Paper: Mercer Management Consulting, UK, 2002.

78 For instance Coca-Cola: A. Hill and B. Liu, 'No Quarter is Given in Executive Dream', *Financial Times,* 16 December 2002.

79 As discussed by Gary Hamel in *Leading the Revolution*, Harvard Business School Press, Cambridge, MA, 2000.

80 Remarks on Amazon's ability to generate revenue through its website know-how, even if it never sells another book, from H. Jung, 'Software is Amazon's Secret Asset', *Calgary Herald*, 7 July 2003.

81 For problems and alternative measures to assess and evaluate new sources of value, see for example R. Srivastava, T. Shervani and I. Fahey, 'Market-Based Assets and Shareholder Value: A Framework for Analysis', *Journal of Marketing*, Vol. 62, 1999; also J. Ivey, 'Accounting for Knowledge', *Corporate Finance*, March 2002.

82 See C. Ittner and D. Larcker, 'Coming up Short on Non-Financial Performance Measurement', *Harvard Business Review*, November 2003.

83 T. Stewart, 'Accounting Gets Radical', *Fortune*, 8 April 2001.

84 J. Daum, for comments on the SEC's and others' attempts in the United States to include intangibles in company valuation, *Intangible Assets and Value Creation*, John Wiley, 2003. For a summary on the status of efforts in the EU see C. Holtham and R. Youngman, 'Measurement and Reporting of Intangibles: A European Policy Perspective', paper presented at the January 2003 Intangibles Conference at McMaster University, Canada. The OECD has also been active in trying to establish a new accounting metric for intangibles; see for instance OECD, *White Paper: Reporting on Intangible Assets*, Paris, 2002; and *White Paper: New Measures for the New Economy*, Paris, 2002.

85 G. Hamel and L. Valikangas talk about the need for organizational resilience in 'The Quest for Resilience', *Harvard Business Review,* September 2003.